THE BOOKS OF "IS"

"FOR THE ASCENSION"
Communion with the Great Mystery
Thru the Baptism of:

The Holy Shekinah": The Divine Feminine

"FOR THOSE WHO ARE READY"

BOOK ONE:

"THE DANCE OF BECOMING"

"STAR WISDOM SEEDS"

(Awakening The Divine Encoded Memories.)

(THE ANCIENT LANGUAGE OF LIGHT AND SOUND)

Quantum wisdom contemplations: messages/teachings, verse and story

IN

*Communion *with the *Creator; *Angels; *Star Relation; *Ancient Ancestors; Spiritual Guides; Mother Earth/ her Spirits; and the *Celestial Hierarchy;*

*'MYSTICISM, *WITH A METAPHORICAL, ESOTERIC AND SHAMANIC NATURE'*

IN THE FORMS OF: CHANNELED:

Wisdom, inspirations, metaphors, parables, verse, & story, including: archetypes, ideograms, Icons, meditative drawings and various other matrices of writings thru the Author

✡ ✡

****

*** ACCESSING: THE AKASHIC RECORD, THE SHEKINAH AND THE ANGELS ***
*** ACCESSING THE SUPER CONSCIENCE/SUPREME-INTELLIGENCE ***
*** STAR NATIONS/ANCESTRAL KNOWLEDGE & WISDOM ***
*** ACCESSING THE SACRED CODES WITHIN ***
*** ACCESSING THE QUATUM HOLOGRAM ***
*** AWAKENING THE DIVINE DNA ***
*** AND MORE! ***

INCLUDING:

Reader's "Co-Authoring": Space For Own In-Spired Writings

WRITTEN BY:

Dr. R. Lowery-Hawk D.D., D.R.S., PhD.

THE BOOKS OF "IS"

BOOK ONE
"THE DANCE OF BECOMING"

For those who seek to know

AuthorHouse™
1663 Liberty Drive
Bloomington, IN 47403
www.authorhouse.com
Phone: 1-800-839-8640

Published by AuthorHouse 8/27/2012
ISBN: 978-1-4670-6062-2 (sc)
ISBN: 978-1-4670-6064-6 (e)

Library of Congress Control Number: 2011919460

DISCLAIMER: These book series do not constitute a claim. The contents may not be misconstrued as direct advice and guidance. The Author makes no claim that any writings in the book series of: THE BOOKS of "IS" are of any now known practicing cultural belief or religion; nor that the readings will guarantee an awakening of any memories, etc. in the reader. Therefore, it is understood that whatever might transpire or not transpire, is the sole responsibility and decision of the reader/purchaser of these books. When purchasing these books, the buyer and reader agrees to indemnity and holds harmless the Author, the publisher, its officers, associates, supply companies, employees, agents, and representatives, safe from all liabilities, expenses and proceedings.

*Author can be contacted for speaking engagements, teaching, workshops and other spiritual matters at:

www.littlemiamiartisans.com/drrlowery
and/or E-mail: equipoise.inquestof@yahoo.com

✡

* * * *

* *

Watch for:

✡ ✡

The Books of "*IS*"
On CD
Coming to you soon!

"Now you can enjoy the powerful and moving benefits of The Books of "IS" even more! Lie back and relax while listening to the gentle, soothing and melodic voice of the Author reading to you, as you travel your Spirit-Soul journey within."

Also
IN THE NEAR FUTURE:

The 2nd Book of:
The Books of "*IS*"

BOOK TWO:

"The Song of Sia"

Look for other books by the Author!

THE DRAWINGS IN THE BOOKS ARE ALSO AVAIABLE SEPARATELY AND IN COLOR
****

* **THE AUTHOR IS AVAILABLE FOR SPEAKING ENGAGEMENTS AND WORKSHOPS**
(See page 171 in back of book for contact information)

...everything on the earth has a purpose,
every disease an herb to cure it,
and every person a mission.
This is the Indian theory of existence.

.--Morning Dove (Christine Quintasket) (1888-1936) - Salish

.... IS

The Honorary Author:

Of the In-Spired Handwritings in this book

DATE: ....

CONTENTS

A BLESSING FOR YOU!

MAY THE LIGHT OF LOVE GUIDE YOU,
MAY YOUR HEART ALWAYS BE TRUE—
MAY THE DANCE ALWAYS MOVE YOU,
AND THE SONG ALWAYS SING THRU—

MAY YOU RECEIVE THE BLESSINGS
THIS BOOK'S PURPOSE
INTENDS TO BRING—
MAY THE MEMORIES OF BECOMING
STIR YOUR INTERNAL SONG
TO ALWAYS SING—

---THE AUTHOR
AUGUST 03, 2011
WEDNESDAY, 9:00 P.M.

"Here in lies
My gift of love,
For the sake of love..."

----The Author
Dr. R. Lowery-Hawk
February 14, 2011

DEDICATED TO THE LOVING MEMORY OF:

DARTANYON

Dartanyon Christopher Obermeyer

My son's son; my Grandson

DEDICATION TO AND FOR:

(MY CHILDREN, GRANDCHILDREN, AND OUR FUTURE GENERATION)

***MY CHILDREN:* Christopher (Chris), Michelle (Shelly), and Leah (Le-Le)**

"Thank you for choosing me for your birth mother. It is my greatest desire that you come to awaken to Truth, understanding and wisdom, AND, Love; realizing and understanding much about the Great Mysteries of life, of you, your life experiences, and its lessons of joy and love; and… of me."

***MY GRANDCHILDREN:* Fantashia (Tashia); Cheyenne (Chy); Saranda; Makayla (Kay-k); & * Dartanyon (Dart).** I compiled these writings in book form for you to have with you, not only something of me and about me, but also so to assist you when the day comes that you choose to open this book and read what I want you to know on the Truth of The Mysteries of Life, and so to pass on to your children, their children, (all generations), and on to others. This is my gift to you and to life:

A gift of Love: a gift to live on!

***(My grandson "Dart's" Spirit is now in the world of Spirit, among the Ancestors and the Angels. He passed to the other side Feb.19/20, in 1999, at the young Earth age of three years and eight months. "We Love you 'Dart' for ever, and *beyond* ever. Our little Angel, our Heart, our 'Star', know that our Love and your Light still shines brightly…)"**

TO THOSE GRANDCHILDREN (AND MY UNBORN CHILD) WHO NEVER SURVIVED TO BIRTH'S FULL TERM; AND TO ALL THOSE FUTURE GENERATIONS YET TO COME TO EARTH :

"We love you in the before, then, now, still and forever.
You are not forgotten; not now, not ever."

To each of my Children and my Grandchildren that are now and later will be:

"I Love each of you in that circle of Love within my heart that never ends. You are my joy, my Love, and my inspiration to be and to do more; to continue to hope, believe, and to Love…
and, Love…and Love and ***live!***

"YOU ARE MY HEART!"

"May these books touch each of you in the way of good; gifting you with a special part of me; for I care deeply for you, and I Love you! We continue on, and therefore, I am with you ALWAYS! May you 'listen' to your 'heart' as you 'sing' the 'stars' inside you to 'dance'. When you do this, there I shall be also, Loving you and guiding you. When you do this, there inside you I shall be, along with your DNA; there among…

"THE MEMORIES…!"

"I LOVE YOU ALWAYS!"

"LOVE NEVER DIES, BUT RATHER, SPIRALS ON AND ON,"

"LOVE FOREVER WITHOUT END…"

**** LAST BUT NOT LEAST: THANK YOU MOM AND DAD! ****
IN WAYS WE MAY NOT HAVE UNDERSTOOD, I HAVE LEARNED MUCH.

In Loving Memory of:
My Mother: Pearl M. Meece, and my Father: Raymond N. Lowery

IN DEDICATION TO:

OUR CREATOR

AND THAT GREAT SPIRAL OF LIFE...
Great Spiral of Light!

"May these writings help 'rock' us back to you, rejoining us in the sacred 'hoop' and sacred "web" as ONE family with many gifts of truth to add to the whole of creation."

✡

* * * *

* *

* *

* *

I'M IN DEDICATION AND DEDICATED TO:

The Great Mystery-Goddess-God, Star Nations, Our Ancestors, The Spiritual Helpers, The Ascended Masters, The Angelic Host, Mother Earth, and all the "unseen" Loving Beings who guided me and assist me, in my life ,

And my mission on Earth.

AND TO

The Re-Call to:

"RE-MEMBERING"

WRITTEN: 2002

"THE SHEKINAH IS DESCENDING, HOLDING THE BLUE DOVE..."

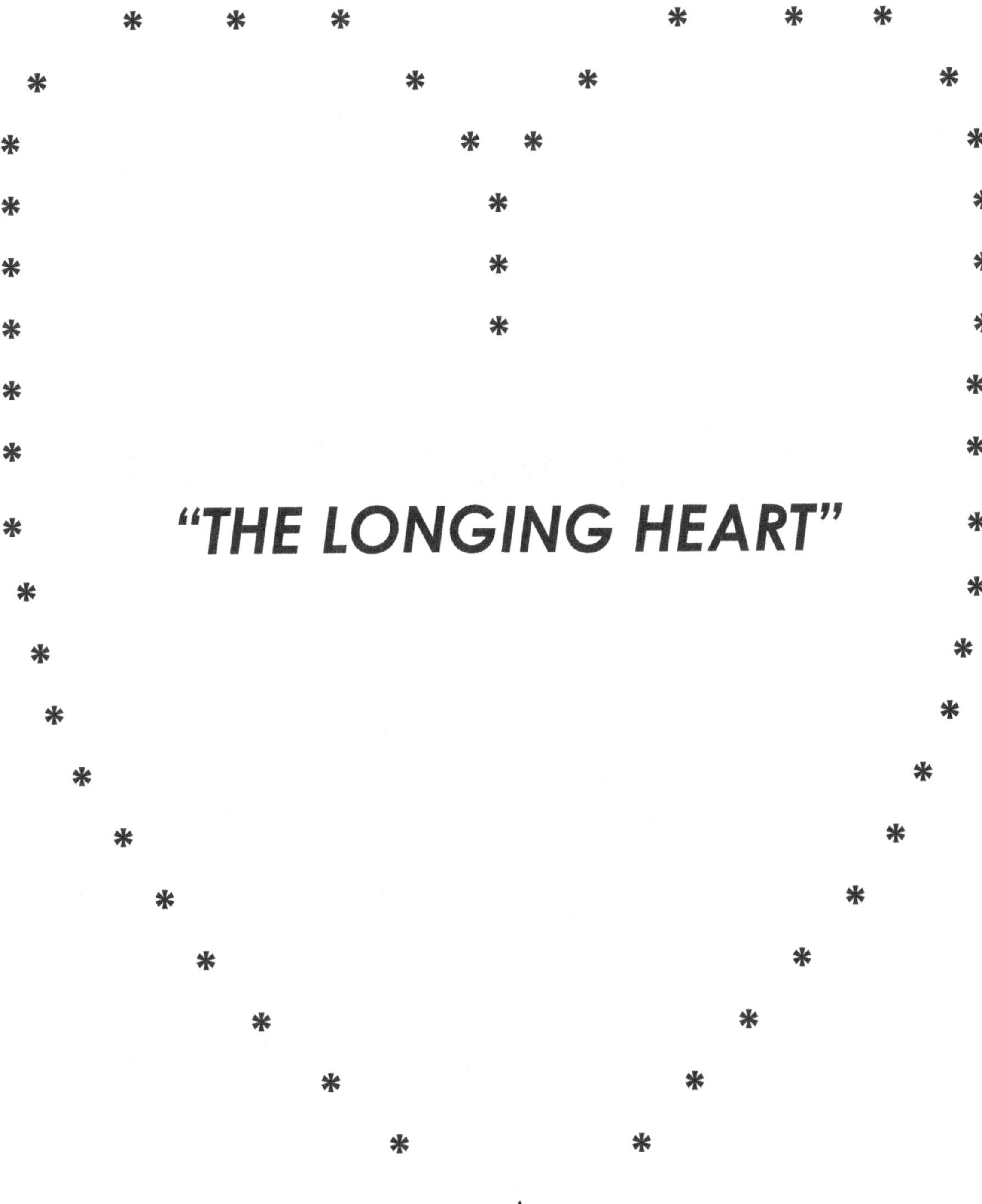

IS THE SOUL STRETCHING…

...And the Spirit SEEKING

---THE AUTHOR
DR. R. LOWERY-HAWK
2011

"FOR THOSE WHO SEEK TO KNOW"

*   *   *   *   *   *

"THE HEART KNOWS"

...AND YOUR SOUL REMEMBERS...

---THE AUTHOR

2011

INTRODUCTION

"The Journey into Your Soul"

"The Secrets"

Dear and Beloved Reader,

My intentions for writing the Books of "IS" are many; all of them are of the best of intensions, for all existence. All intensions are for guiding you to The "Awakening": the realization of who you truly are, and your purpose of existence; in hopes of bringing us all back into unity, for the betterment of life in its purest form of Love and Joy. For we are all related! We are all in a matrix web of one. We affect one another and everything! We are one! These various writings are one of many different ways of assisting you to your awareness in this "Dream". What is the "Dream"? What am I talking about? This book and your going into contemplation with it, learning how to apply it to all life around you and in your time of dreaming (in the time of your bodies nightly, or/and daily sleep time for the body), will assist you in realizing that your third dimensional world, is a "dream"/an illusion. You along with everyone else are creating this "dream", this illusion.

This book, I, along with the Celestial Hierarchy, (In their many Heavenly and Star names/definitions) will attempt to "awaken" you so you will know and remember what you hold inside you; that which was given to you, encoded in you; that which you are and always have been, and have held recorded since the beginning of creation.

I have been receiving Divine Messages for more than fifty-eight years. The writings in this book, except where noted, and the drawings, are "channeled" through me, given to me, by the Ancient Ancestors and the Heavenly Hierarchy of Love that go by many names, by many people. These writings have been written down over a spanned period of twenty-eight years. Before this I just recognized them as Truths...as an Innate

Knowing that seemed natural, and then proved themselves to be true. Then in 1984, I received the message telepathically from those of The Higher Realms, to write these "Knowings" and Messages down; put into books, and have them published. (There are more of these writings. They will be put in future books.) After receiving these messages over a long period of time I began to understand who I am and who WE are. I began to understand more about the discord we experience and why. In the eighties the Star Relations told me more about myself. They told me things during my "Awakening" time and also in my body's Sleep-Dream-Time. They gave me a name that was more like an explanation of who I am, rather then just one word as most names are. It is my Spirit's name. It is the best I can say about it at this time.

Many of you are feeling changes within your self and seeing it in others around you as the Earth is going through her changes. The Earth is also you, and all that are upon her, within her, and around her. She is also the elements. This means the weather as well as the vibrations from her and within her, such as quakes. All this is affecting the other planets as well as all upon her. You are going through a type of healing crisis, a purification of Divine light. These Higher "Healing" Energy frequencies are necessary for the restoration of her original intended and created condition and purpose. We too, being part of her, are going through this as well. We must stay calm, loving and joyful during this transaction. She is giving "birth" to her Purer Self, as are we. We are moving into a Higher Frequency, another Higher Dimension, and HAVE arrived in a Higher Frequency that is moving faster into higher ones yet, and so, we are feeling and experiencing a healing crisis. We are ascending into a Higher Light of Love. Do not be afraid. It is a natural adjustment occurrence. A natural adjustment aided by Loving and Caring Star Relations, Angelic Beings and the Planets/Beings in our galaxy. Therefore we are also aided by what many refer to as the Galactic Federation. We are being cleansed on a cellular level. Our cellular memories and our DNA is being cleansed of all that has held us back from the perfection we are and are always moving towards: (The Creating Source) LOVE!

These writings and drawings are contemplative. They have a pattern, a rhythm and arrangement that will bring about a light acceleration within you. This Light is The Light of Love, and is send from The Shekenah (Holy Spirit) and the higher realms to assist you in your awareness of truth and those who are assisting us in our ascension to a Higher Realm of Light and Sound, which is what and who we are: Beings Of Light and sound; "Children"-Of-Light-And-Sound (Song). All things Sing. These writings are to "Sing" to you and "awaken" you to the Truth of That and you; to "waken" you to your beauty that is in union with all beauty, harmony, Light, and Love. Your True Self is so beautiful, and your True Home sings a Love Song of such beauty that it is beyond description! May the "Light-Seeds" of these Light-Sounds Writings (Light-Songs) and drawings (Memory Codes) awaken you to your True Self and True "Home". Some of my intentions may seem redundant, but the redundancy has its purpose in the "remembering".

When you read and view the drawings, go about it relaxed and calm. Do not rush. Then when you have read and viewed them all, go back for repeated readings and drawing contemplations. Different things will unfold for you. I will be creating a CD with my voice, of this book and also future books. I will also create a special journal for your personal Insights for the future. Meanwhile I have created a few pages in this book for you to use as a personal journal of your Awakening Insights, creating a co-author affect. This then is your own personal book of awakening. Enjoy!

** If at some point you wish to skip some of the introduction and return back to it later, I suggest you go to the prelude and read it, then return to read the rest of the introduction at a later time. But do read the introduction. Read ALL of this book; it is put together and written to create a vibration that works with your neurons, cells, and DNA so to stir your Light within, allowing the Shekinah to descend in Holy Divine Light, and so, enabling you to connect with your Divine Higher Self/Over-Soul and The Beings Of Love, Light And Sound. They will assist you in your ascension and the releasing into your consciousness your Divine and Ancient Memories.*

I wish now at this time to give you a "Channeled" Message. I will now channel my Higher Self, speaking to you from that place of my Star Being, from two of the Star Nations of the Galactic Federation: our Star Relations:

"We, of the Morning Star, from the Sacred Flame of the New Day, and those of the Evening Star of the Sacred Night, greet you. We welcome you to the dawning of a new era. We welcome you to the discovery of the "Seeds" "planted" in the pages of this book, and those that are "planted within you". The world you have been experiencing in this space and time continuum is lifting into another "mirror" of Purer Light. We, of the Star Nations, along with other Celestial Beings, are sending "Star Seeds" of Light to you and your world: "The Lost Continent Of The Stars": the "World-Of-Three"; the world you call: Earth. This world as you know it is changing. Becoming a marvel to behold! All upon Earth are ascending to another level of "Light". To another mirrored facet of the many worlds that make up creation as a whole. The "time" has arrived for the releasing of the "Word". The Word is the language of Light and Sound. The Word is Truth. Truth is Light. Light is Sound and beyond your present awareness. The Word is Supreme Intelligence: The Essence and The Light comprising all that IS That, which you call: "God" (the completeness of all energies as one). To reach you, so to protect this planet and you as a human species, we are participating in its (and your) deliverance from the bondage of forgetfulness and illusion. You have been cloaked in "darkness", and ignorance for more time than you can understand at this period of your existence on this plane, this Star: Earth. We, of the other Stars

that you sometimes call planets, worlds, or multi-dimensions and heavens, have been working with your DNA; your cells; and the neurons in your brain, and those neurons in your "gut" and your heart. Your DNA connects and affects all things on this world, and beyond. We reach your neurons and DNA by Light and Sound. We then "stir" Light and Sound of Melodic Frequencies to move inside you, stirring you to poetic words, song, and movements. This is The Dance of Sound and Light that shall lift you into a frequency of ascension in awareness. We, from the Stars, are stirring your "Stars" within you, and those above your planet, into the "dancing up" of The Memories of Creation, and all that it and you truly are, and are meant to realize, then, co-create. The words in this book come from all of us to you, as Seeds of Knowledge and Wisdom, to prime you to The Recall of what is to be recalled, to assist in the ascension of this plane of existence. All that is known in Creation is like a story within a story. A Spiraling Never-Ending-Story Of Creation and all the experiences of all creation, unfolding in Memories; Climbing-Spiral-Dancing up The Sacred Tree Of Life...all encoded within all existence. The term story does not have to mean a tale of impossibilities nor improbabilities. Stories are what make up you, and are comprised from ALL experience of all that IS, throughout all that IS, was, and ever shall be. Stories are like pictures in your mind, your visions, and imagination, coupled with possibilities and probabilities. Your mind sees in pictures and symbols. The mind communicates by way of Light and Sound. Stories are a Language Of Light And Sound, which incorporates both sides of your brain, bringing you into balance and to a place of peace and "Somewhere". That "Somewhere" is a place beyond the "heaviness" of limitless thinking and beyond the disbelieve in something that is more enlightening, and beyond your present understanding and memory. It is "Something" in the "Somewhere" that is more then what many feel and believe this life they are experiencing IS. Many people here, in this third world dimensional existence on the planet known by its inhabitants as Earth, are experience life in a darkened state of reality. But the real is beyond that, more then that. It is a continuality of Love that is like a Great Mystery to you. You then sometimes refer to that vastness of life and its knowledge and power, that goes beyond your comprehension, as The Great Mystery: "The-Beyond-The-Beyond, Beyond..." In this book, and the future Books of "IS", "stories" stands for several things. Two of these are: experiences and memories from Creator, creation and Specie-"Tribal"-Groups as far back as the beginning of "Every-thing", and on forward to present moment. When you view the word: stories, in a metaphoric (comparable, parable, symbolic picture quality) way, you will receive other realizations of the deeper truths of what the term: stories implies and brings to your conscience. You become instinctively aware of innate knowledge, understanding and wisdom; "stores" (stories) of... All then, are made up of

stores of "stories" stored inside your DNA and cells. Stored in your body! Stories meant to be shared and compared, in the process of uniting again in "heart", in mind, soul and spirit: in love; by uniting the "We are one" connectiveness of: US! : ONE CREATION; ONE CREATOR. ONE... Know we are here to assist and align you harmoniously, just as planets align, thus creating a frequency that affects all other life. You are affecting us with your disharmony and so we are here to adjust you with your home planet and the other planets natural adjustment that is now taking place and always periodically takes place. This will assist in a gentler transition from one state of becoming to the natural Becoming-Transition of the Light Frequency "upgrading" you and your world are naturally moving into. Those you refer to as the Arch Angels, Seraphim, and Cherubim, along with many other Beings Of Light, are assisting this planet and the life upon her. We are sending down Light Rays Of Understanding to you. These rays are waves of multi-colored Sound and Light. They are Sound-Dancing. They are enfolding you, embracing you, and comforting you in an Angel-Winged Embrace Of Love. The Wave-Of-Under-Standing is descending so to lift you Heart-Ward into Love, wisdom, knowledge, and Truth. Remember your joy and Love. Remember your "Dance and Your Song" it unites you with the Stars and the Creator! Remember the Love..."

I, the Author of this book, cannot give, (nor do I have, yet, in my knowing awareness), all-of-the-ALL, to you, nor share as much as I'd love to with you. Nor does, or can, any one person in the short life span we are experiencing here in these third dimensional-world bodies. I would ask that those who are "hearing" the "Call" that is bringing into their awareness the desire, and drive, to know more and to become more of their Creator given-existence's right, to again Become, and remember. Each of you having then, activated the "Some-things" of a Loving nature, peace, harmony, and unity; compelling them to be of this, about this, and to share this with others; I encourage you to do so. The writings compiled in this book are my own Higher Channeled "Stories" of various kinds. I have however, included several quotes from others, which I came across, AFTER, I had compiled my writings into this book. I decided to use them due to the quotes similarities and their usefulness/validation in the purpose of this book. I have included in the annotations in the back of the book, the reference of the quotes with each one, other wise, all other writings in this book are original, coming forth through me. I encourage you to share your Insights and "Stories". Writing them down, and then contemplating on them, as you are intended to do in the Inspired Writings section of this book, is a great way to connect to the Inner Spirit, the Shekinah-Mother-Holy (that goes by many other names). With that connection a path will be "laid" to the "Heavens" and the "Gate" shall open that will allow truths to unfold. Writing, art, creating, and contemplation, puts us in touch with our Soul, enabling us to see "Who" and "What" we truly are. It assists us in connecting with our "Heart" and our Inner Divine Heart "Fire", creating a direct line with our Higher Self and the "All" of Creator; enabling us then, to unlock the truths encoded, not only within US, but also within ALL Creation. In the Ancient Indigenous Earth (all our Ancestor's) times, stories were mostly oral, but, some were drawn: pictures, or symbols, representing words: a Pictoric Language. But a language it was. It communicated in a Universal Language. This provided a communion, and commonality with all who could understand, or "tap" into the symbolic language. This is what this book is attempting to provide and accomplish. The language of right brain: "feminine": creative, instinctive side, (the symbols and pictures); and left brain: "masculine": logical and mathematical, doubting and inquiring, (their coming together puts the contemplative "pieces-of-the-puzzle-mystery" together). Today, in this "time" of many earth changes and time and space quickening, we are in a great need to quickly remember and return to our connective-ness to the Earth, to the Creator of ALL that IS, and to the Great Spirit, (which goes by many different names) that resides within us and within all life. Because of this quickening-acceleration in our earth, we too, as part of her, are also accelerating, and so this requires accelerated yet calm loving activities and methods. Writing is one method. Artwork and any activity you love that are neither of a selfish nature, nor of a nature to bring about harm to self, anyone or any-thing, are other methods of achieving this. Create the beauty of love in all that you do, believe, think, feel, and say. This is the Golden Elixir of Life that we are to give back to others, to the earth, the moon, the sun, the stars, to other worlds, and on beyond the beyond to the FIRST: that which we refer to as our Loving Supreme Creator; God-Goddess of All Creation that exist beyond our present realization since the beginning! It is the Sacred Circle! It is our "Give-Away"! By giving it, it comes back to us, completing a circuit, a full circle " 8 ": a Sacred Hoop Of Eternity.

None of my writings are meant to be about religion; nor are they pertaining to a particular spiritual belief system; nor about achieving only one particular way of spiritually connecting; nor are they a religion, or pertaining to a particular religion. They are just "Seeds": "Tools", "Sacred tools", of Gentle Reminders. Please use them with the consideration and the intention of love they are intended for. Do not use them without careful thought and choice of your intentions and use. Make those intentions and uses a consideration of how it will affect all people, and all life as a whole. Let it be for the Highest Good and Love for ALL! Look at these writings not only literally, but also in a metaphoric way so to derive many Truths, from each of the writings. Many of the writings are literal, while others may be both or one of the other. It is for you, the reader, to intuitively know, or, receive what is meant for you personally to perceive and receive. In compiling these Quantum Spiritual Writings of The Mysteries of Life, and their ways of bringing The Gifts of Love and Peace, I hope to assist you into taking quiet time to contemplate and to think and sense and create Love. I hope by your doing this, aided by these writings, you will be assisted in "awakening" your own "Stories", Insights, and

*Knowing that you carry inside of you; your "Stories", your "Songs", that "Sing" to you, "asking" to be brought forth into your "Dancing" Conscience-"Awakening-Awareness". As I have said, inside each of us are "Stories": "Seed Stories" of long, long ago; Cellular "Stories" of Memories collected by The Particles of Creation, living within: your cells and your RNA/DNA, living within YOU! Living within ALL life! My purpose, again, in compiling these writings, making them available to you, is so you can enjoy and benefit from them in a good way for yourself, others, the planet, and the Universe: for all life in totality. I wish to enlighten you and others, in hopes of bringing you out of "darkness": bondage of chaos, confusion, hopelessness, ignorance, anger, shame, guilt, fear, despair, and other negative illusions, and into more realization of the Light and its Truths; and into Understanding, so to aid you in aiding and "working" with the Light. I hope to help bring us all back into awareness and Sacred Memory's Attunement to The Great Mystery, The Heavens and Earth; to have others add their Light for The Betterment of mankind and all creation. This is my intention and purpose. "It is also my intention, in my writings and art work, plus all else I do, to help children and adults to remember their importance, their Special-ness, and who they truly are: **Children of the Most High Light**, who we call: A part of God, our Creator. God, that Loving Source, is beyond male and female as we experience and think those terms and genders stand for. This "God-Goddess": the Higher Power Source, is beyond that Male-God or Female-Goddess Principal called whatever one wishes to refer to "GOD" as. (I use the word God in my writings, in reference to the ALL Creating Force/Source of bliss, peace, harmony, balance, and Love, that all things "stem" from and that resides in ALL things.) Many people refer to this Higher Power as: Male and Female Energy: God/Goddess; The Word/The Breath; The Christ/The Light; The Shekinah:(The Holy Spirit/Holy Ghost/Great Spirit/Shekinah. Titles, that in ancient text are considered aspects of the Feminine principle/nature of the Creator), or any of the numerous other titles, that still cannot touch upon all that ALL IS and cannot be named! This ALL, this **IS-NESS**, is a Mystery to us here in this Third Dimensional Plane of Existence. This is why so many of us refer to the **GOD-GODDESS** of ALL **IS-ness** and all creation that ever was, IS, and ever shall be, as: The Great Mystery! I also wrote this book because, those Messengers of "God" who are in the most High Places, that some refer to as: The Heavens, The Star Nations, The Galactic Federation, Other Dimensions, and Spirit Worlds, gifted me this "Language", these Messages, directing me to deliver them to the world, just as they have been directing many others besides myself to do. I had chosen, many years ago, before entering this body, to assist these Divine Beings with the raising of our Loving Light Frequencies so to help human-kind and this powerful round Mother-being, we refer to, here, as: Earth... Earth is humankind's "Ship"; humankind's true material body, humankind's body's "Mother". Earth is your Spirit's (the Real and True You) vehicle and means to experience the affects of the "Dream": life's separation into dualities (light and dark, plus opposites) on this plane of existence, thereby learning about Love and Creation,* *sending back information to the one True Source (God-Force). This sharing of experiences with Creator: All life "below" and "above", creates the "perfect" plan for all creation existing and is becoming ever more. These writings are intended to assist you gently, yet quickly into your True Self, activating your "KNOWING" and "rocking" you Lovingly "awake" in conscious, in the embrace of the Holy Spirit: Shekinah, The Feminine Essence of Creator). This is to be done so that the Earth's Great Purification, the transition into the "New" Earth Body (which is another dimension of a Higher Vibrating Frequency for her and for you as a body/unit, and your conscience-ness.), will be easier for you, so you can transcend and be lifted up into The Higher Christ-Serpentine-Light that the "Angels" are assisting in pouring forth and down upon the Earth, thus, upon us. It is important that each of us thinks, speaks, feels, does, and creates ALL things of peace and Love. It is important we "activate" our "Feminine Nature" of intuition, compassion, and creativity, creating things we Love to do, and envision the world we wish to live in, in a way that is compassionate, loving, gentle, forgiving, peaceful, calm, and thoughtful towards the planet, and towards others; but also, towards one's Self. By going within, where you can be still and at peace, centering your focus not on fear but on Love, doing kindness, being forgiving, and learning how to express this; contemplating on what you enjoy doing and creating, you then shall connect with The Great Creator and this Planet; thereby activating a "Open Door": a Portal for the Shekinah to descend upon you in the Baptism Form that appears like a "Blue Dove" descending. She then activates the Shekinah-Holy Spirit within you. This rises up making a pathway to the Golden Gate". This Portal, "Door" or "Gate" or "Wormhole" will await your "knock" (if that be YOUR choice.) For it will be your choice whether to venture further on the path or to "pause", or to turn away. After one "Knocks" one eventually is "Knocked Back". Do not be discouraged. This "Knocking back" (purification with trials and tests) is to allow all that makes up you to decide if you are now truely ready, and, WILLing to "embrace" ALL of you, by way of learning to "Dance" with your "Shadow". "The "Shadow" I am metaphorically referring to is those negative thoughts, feelings and beliefs you have heard, experienced, then come to believe throughout life and thus, hold as real, and which are not of the "Spiraling Dance" of love for Self, others, and all life. These "Shadowers" are the polluted "Things" you hold inside you, and inside your mind that hold you back from The Light, even though you may not be consciously aware of them or that they do. The "Dance" is the movement of awareness into the acknowledgment of these "Shadows" Of Light that need understood and moved into the Pure Light, releasing you to the knowledge and wisdom of what lessons it brought you for the betterment of Soul. But you have free will: free decision, free choice. If you choice to go forward into the seemly unknown towards the Light of Truth, "She" then will "open" the "Golden Gate" to the "Higher Heavens" that leads to the Over-Soul, and to the Supreme Intelligence: The "Male" Aspect of God. "Wheels-Within-Wheels" shall then "spin", drawing with them a "Golden-Spiraling-Ladder" that shall reach "upwards" towards the "Heavens". It will enable you to "climb it" to that "Golden Gate" that opens to the Supreme ONE Mind with its all knowing completeness of wisdom, understanding and Truth; uniting all Things eternally as ONE complete and continuous Knowing. This Spiraling-Golden- "Serpent"-(Serpentine)-"Ladder" is your DNA. The Wheels-Within-Wheels are your Body's "Gateways" Of Energy/Light Circuits that spin The Life Force throughout your body. (These "Wheels" are referred to by many as: Charkas). There, the Shekinah, joined with the Supreme Intelligence, shall guide you and commune with you. The Shekinah, Holy Spirit, aligns you thirteen charkas up, and further yet, connecting you with your Higher Self, The Galactic and Angelic Helpers/Messengers, and The Supreme Mind. If you choose to utilize this in a good way for ALL life, you then shall Light Travel higher, and access more on the way of Sacred Truth and its Wisdom. Use it wrongly and you will have only succeeded in creating a great disturbing chaos for yourself; a chaos in which not only shall you have to spend many "Hellish Lessons" in experiencing its affect on the Whole Of Creation, BUT also, you will have to experience individually how it affected the life of each that it has "harmed"! So use any and all sources you read, learn, access, teach, think, feel, hear, speak, and do, for the best for all life and, for Love…I offer this book and all in it, in a good way, with those intentions, to each of you. Please know that none of the material in this, or future books, I write, is guaranteed to bring all I have said about. All will depend upon you and the Higher Power of Love that we come from and are returning to. The material in this book and any future books I may write, will, however, give you the opportunity to make the free willed decision, the choice, whether they can and are assisting you on your path. They will help assist you when and in the way you are ready to understand them and apply them. At different times in your spiritual growth the material may bring to you new insights, as you are ready. I have turned this all over to the Creator of Love, peace, and life, along with the Creator's Loving and assisting Messengers of Truth, Light, Peace, and Love, to assist each of you in the way that is best for your Divine Highest Good, and the welfare of each and all. May this be so! I realize that these things I say in this introduction, and the writings here in, may come across as possibly strange, false and even delusional to the many who have never heard such things, or who have never experienced or learned of these Ancient Mysteries Of Truths of life, The Great Mystery, and our beginnings, etc. These Ancient Mysteries of Truth have been reserved and gone "underground" for protection throughout the ages, being revealed to only those who are meant/chosen to know and use them to assist humankind, for the purpose of Harmonic Love and Light's continuality of Harmonious Creations in The Circle Of Life, (all that is and will be created) These teachings, these "Secrets" on Truth of Existence and Creator, are now being brought forth to give again to human kind, for mankind's (human kind) benefit. "Man" is in a period of existence, here in this Dimensional World, of great need for these well-guarded Truths of a deeper comprehension and nature, to be brought back to*

"Her/Him". This Understanding, this Wisdom, this Knowledge: these Truths of Creation, have been Spiritually protected and guarded for over thousands of years; cleverly concealed in Sacred Text and Literatures, and oral stories, handed down as "stories" or song/poetry, revealing themselves only to those who have the "Ear To Hear", and the "Eyes to See". For, it is these who will assist in the "up lifting" of "Man-kind" to the Father's and Mother's (God/Goddess) "embrace and abode". Many clever and wise ways were these Mysteries, these Secrets, "hidden"...there, yet seeming NOT there. Truths, yet seeming NOT true...except to those viewed and called by those in the Heavenly Abode, answering, willing the call back to Love and Pure Light, and to the assisting with the cleansing away of "stagnated energies" and attaching inities, transforming them into Beauty-Light. These "Chosen Ones" are willing to assist in the transforming of "darkness" and the bringing of more Pure Light to the places and life that needs it. These Secret Mysteries, now being brought forth again and concealed in The Books of "IS", were always well protected and revealed only to those who were willingly and spiritually prepared by the Creator of us All through the Creator's Angels, and who then proved ready to understand them and willing to use them in the way they were intended to be used: in peace, Love and Unity of Light with ALL creation, in ALL Universes, for the Highest Good for ALL Existence. I do not wish you to believe anything you do not wish to believe, nor feel you should believe. Your journey in the Universal Flow of Life is yours, along with your choices. I honor your Spirit and those choices of your unfoldment of returning to The Light of "God", your Creator. I hope you will honor mine, and those others who have been given these Sacred Truths, these "Keys" to The Heavens, delivered by the Angels and High Beings. If you disagree with what we know is true, remember and be about Love and gentleness, exercising the ways of the Loving Spirit of "God" and the Holy Spirit of ALL Love within you and within us and within all things. Let your ways and actions be of goodness and non-violence for ALL people and ALL life as you disagree, IF you disagree, rather then being one of fear, violence, dark judgment and the using of the word and actions to inflict harm by you and others to those you disagree with; do not understand; and/or fear or feel uncomfortable with. For if you come from those ungodly thoughts, emotions, words, and actions you are creating more darkness and more damage for Self and ALL Creation; for you will be creating the opposite of Love Peace and Light of the God you think and say you are about; and therefore will be creating the evil you say you are against.

Again, this introduction may seem redundant at times, but it is so to help you to see the many reasons for and intentions of such a book. It is also so you will recall and feel the message I am trying to bring forth in a good way, for a good cause, for you and the universe. You are loved and protected by the Light of "God", knowing this, may you relax into that Love and protection; and may you receive understanding and gain guidance from the Creator Of Love...of us all, to the Truths as you are ready and willing to receive them. I then hope that this book, and anything else I can do, will contribute in helping others to reunite in Love, compassion and empathy for one another and this planet that feeds and supports us. I hope this book shall encourage you, the reader, to think, feel, explore and contemplate upon your Self, others, all of our relatives of nature, Creator God-Goddess, our Spirit Helpers, this Planet and Truth. It is my hope that the writings and drawings in ***The Books of "IS"*** *shall encourage you to also question, and explore; and in silence, ponder the world around you, and within you, with the intention, (your intention) being to re-unite with the Sacred Hoop of the Great Mystery's Loving Light; thereby, mending it and bringing it "back together" with ALL life. May this be so! I hope to bring into your awareness, the fact that you can "tap" into the "ALL KNOWING" by way of Love and peace in nature; prayer; silence; meditation; contemplation; questioning and inquiring; and, gifting... Giving back! You can attune to Spirit and Life, including the All Creator, by going "within yourself" and preparing a Loving place there, seeking... Beauty Of Life and Self shall open for you when you "listen" to your "Heart-of-Hearts", that place of The Holy Of Holies, where the Holy Spirit dwells above, within you, and, within ALL things/life! The Higher Truths open when one "opens their Heart". Yet, no amount of reading about Higher Truths will open and be useful to you unless your Heart is opened so you can seek within. All Truths are within you for The Great Creator put them there as a Special "Secret Place" to not be "lost". This then* ***IS THE "SECRET".***

Dear Reader, yes, my intentions here, in all I have said and done with this book and the future books, are to assist in that "opening" of your Heart to the Human Soul's and Spirit's "Remembering" and then bringing about ***"The-Sacred-Marriage-of-the-Two".*** *I'm attempting to do this by bringing into your Awareness-Enlightenment on the Truth of Creation, life, yourself, and all that you and we are; and all that we are meant to know; and* ***all we are becoming****. My desire then, is to also assist "The-Little-Ones": The "Children" which are you who yet do not recall the Truths, and those "Children" that are now in infant and Child-Bodies, and the "Children" of the future, who will be arriving on this Earth, becoming what the Future Human Race shall be...*

I have enclosed in the prelude more on the introduction of my books, their goal, and the importance of each person to unite in Love, remembering who they truly are and their purpose. This importance is not only to and for you, but also to and for the Circle of Life! This introduction and the prelude is then, also, A "Teaching,

"A Story" Of Truth:

In Love and Light---
The Author

PRELUDE

"Once we were close to Our Creator, and to Spirit and Soul. We were close to Mother Earth, all creatures, all things, and... to one another... We once knew of our connective-ness and honored it, balanced it, and grew with it into Harmonic Ever-Creating-Beauty. Then, a "Darkness" came, descending the people into a kind of "sleep". Many forgot their Truth and forgot The Sacred Instructions. They forgot their Divine Connective-ness and their Sacred Path; and...they forgot their Sacredness... They "lost" their Ancestral Memories and lost sight of their Spirit and its link with the Great Mystery and Mother Earth (Union of Spirit and Matter). It is my purpose here, to assist you, the reader, in re-gaining your connection and realization of the Sacredness of Life and You; of your Divinity and connection with it and all that has been, and shall be created by the Supreme Intelligence, who many refer to as: The Great Mystery, God/Goddess...Source-Of-All-Things, and our Creator. It is my purpose to help you re-member all that is good and true...(all that has been "lost"...) My goal is for you to learn in a relaxing, enjoyable, entertaining, and yet powerful way...by way of contemplation and rhythm; a journey into yourself, by way of obtaining the Eternal Music Of The Spheres; a journey returning "Home" to, and into, your Over-Soul, so to set it to "dancing" with your Spirit and your Divine DNA/RNA. I hope to bring you to the Eternal Music Of The Spheres. The Eternal Music Of The Spheres is a high vibrating Light/Sound, also referred to as the "Singing of The Angels" by True Mystics. The Ancient Philosophers and Mystics say this Light-Sound-Song "stirs up" and creates in abundance, the Pure Light, revitalizing the Seven Sacred Energy (Life Force) Centers ("Gates/Charkas/Wheels") of the body of ALL Creatures and the Planet, and on to The Universe. This Light brings Spiritual Comprehension, filling the body and illuminating the mind, dispelling ignorance. It puts you in contact with the Akasha and The KNOWING. The Akasha is also known as the Akashic Records, The Place Of Records/Memories; The Golden Grid; The Matrix; The Mass Unconscious; The Crystal Grid; The Book Of Life; Records Of The Soul/Over-Soul/Higher-Self; Hologram; and other various names. The Akasha, by the Ancients, is also known, as The Plasma---(the formless breath before crystallized form: matter). Could the Akasha then be The Supreme Mind, The Super Intelligence, The Father Principle? As the Plasma, The Formless "Breath", stirred up and created Spirals, it then created Cosmic "Wind". This "Wind", this "Breath", was Spirit. Spirit was The Word, The Logos. It is said that all can be made known to us when we are ready. Creation is a Mystery to us, for it goes beyond our understanding at this time. Mystics say that perhaps if we advanced in The Sound and Light: The Eternal Music/Song, we'd stir the "Stars" up to "dancing", and by doing so, we'd stir up the Internal "Stars" and Song;

thus, illuminating our minds with more Light. We, perhaps, then, would raise the "Matter" we occupy, in the way of our "Flesh"---Body, to a higher frequency and so gain more awareness of these Life Mysteries. It is not enough however, to gain knowledge without the responsibilities that go with it. Therefore, wisdom must enter in to gain true knowledge, understanding, and its application; gaining then, deeper truths. This comes by intering The Silence, but also by way of experiencing. These experiences then become tests, "lessons" or "teachers". Like a student in a classroom, life tests us in its "school" of life to let us see how well we have learned, and if we have leaned importantly and wisely enough to move on to receiving more answers of Truth and the "Gifts" earned by these lessons, along with their disciplined nature. This then also determines one's readiness to move to more revealing answers of Truth. These experiences move us forward, and the wisdom and understanding learned from them moves us "upward". This is like a dance... a gyrating, spiraling dance of becoming more, in every way. The writings in the book series: The Books of "IS" are versions of "Music"/"Song"---Sound and Light: The Eternal Music, to assist you in setting your Soul, through your Spirit, to "singing", and so "stir up" your "Light-Body", resulting in your Spirit and Soul "singing" and "dancing" as partners, becoming one. Thereby, you enter and "hear" "The Eternal Song Of The Spheres", and there, access your Soul's Records: The Akasha-Book-O-f-Life-Records-Of-The-Divine-ALL-That was and IS, "stepping" then into:

The KNOWING.

Studies have shown that the gut has more neurons then the brain. The gut is said to be a "brain". We get gut messages---impressions; and when our stomach is upset it is said that it is because of the senses it picks up. With this in mind, we should then take more seriously the feelings we receive there. We should become more aware and learn how to trust these feelings. Our Dear and precious planet Earth has a Collective Conscience and Memory "Bank". She collects thought forms and actions: energy movements/blue-prints/impressions. She records the actions and the re-actions into her "Bones": The S/tone People (which are also The Family of Crystals). She does this, working with the Universe, The Great Mystery (God/Goddess---Life Force), to cycle and re-cycle these energies out and back again to you and to ALL life, for to "taste" (sample), experience and thus, learn from, so to create by deciding (choosing) on a conscience and subconscious level: Do we keep or change it? How does it feel? How does it act and re-act with our "Dance" (patterns of movements: our actions, our becoming of more Light) that we have created thus far? How does it affect that "Dance" and our life? How does it sound/feel and move (Dance) with our Becoming "Song" (Sound/Energy/Light) pattern and blue print we are ALL creating all of the time?

What is best for our upward frequency Light goal? All this affects the third and forth dimension, and moves on up affecting all other dimensions as well, due to that movement to those Higher Frequencies/Dimensional Worlds. Manifestation occurs here on Earth, The Third Dimensional World we now occupy, as well as on other Dimensions; most of us just aren't aware of that yet. We then create what we hold as true here on this plane of existence. We create what we think, feel, see and experience as real, to be our truth. We continuously create our world and our life with our thoughts: (imaginings, visions, beliefs, thought forms of energy vibrations); our words: (sound, speech, vibrations); our emotions: (feelings, adrenaline, actions, reactions, expressions, vibrations); our physical: (actions, reactions, movements, habits). Do we become more in harmony with ALL creation, or do we destroy more? Do we destroy more of the balance of creation/life then we add balance to the Symphony of: The Creation Song And Dance of Becoming? We, human beings, as a species, too, have a Collective Conscience and thus, Collective Memories. Collective Memories: "Blue Print", if you will, as a species, but also, as a Spirit and Soul from the Divine-Super-Conscience-Spirit-Soul that creates ALL Creation. We have what many refer to as a Super Conscience. Our Super Conscience is connected to the Highest Conscience of ALL: the "Higher Power"; The Over-Soul; The Life Force; The Great Mystery; The Great Spirit; The Creator; The Goddess/God Force of ALL Creation; The 'Ruler'; The Lord; The Creator of ALL THAT IS...The I AM; The We are; The IS; The Everything and The Ever-Will-Be, for, Everything IS. We are everything, and ALL is there and here, for ALL IS present. This Higher Conscience IS and KNOWS ALL! "IS" can be thought of then as: Present Realization...

PRESENCE OF:

**** I realizing the Source of I am: I exist.****

**** I realizing the Source of ALL: I seek all that I am.****

**** I realizing the Source of becoming: I become more like creator ****

**** I realizing the Source of my Being-ness in the present moment.****

**** I realizing that Source IS everything, and IS as it IS realized and believed to be****

**** In Webster's Dictionary two of his definitions of IS are: ****

****1. The present tense of be; 2. Third person singular ****

*

Therefore, "IS" could possibly stand for singularity, oneness, and the affirming of your present world of becoming and being-ness; realizing that the person/s responsible for changing their world and life's outcome is each of us, each one of us, coming together in singularity, Oneness. The 3rd person singular could also be like the 3rd point of a Divine Trinity and the 3rd point of the Trinity of existence, such as: Father+Mother=Child; Supreme Mind/Intelligence (Masculine Principle)+Holy Spirit (Shekinah: Feminine Principle)=Conscious Awareness (Logos, The "Word", The Christ; The Child Offspring);

thought+movement (action)=Manifested Creation; hot+cold=warm; black+white=gray. When we look at it this way, we possibly might understand that the number three: The Trinity; is in ALL manifestation. Realizing this, we might then come to realize the importance of becoming more aware and "awaken" to the IS-ness reality (realizing) of the becoming of the return of the third person singularity, and the living in the moment, which is the true existence. It IS The Present-ness of Truth and The Real. We then must "awaken" once more to The IS-ness Reality (I exist in the present-realizing), as The Third Person Singular, the Spirit within that manifested into form: Crystallized Plasma. We aim for to return to singularity, but not as a singular that "sings" and "dances" alone, but as a trinity unit that has been created as one whole and complete unit for life's expansion and continuality, given a singular choice and will to become aware and know, then "sing, and dance" in this world of sensory perception and illusionary plasma, painting on the "art board" of co-creating. Then having done so, rise up our Light's high frequency to enable us to return to the Divine Trinity, blending and becoming That which we sought. Therefore, IS means many things, too many to grasp yet the totality of it all. For IS also means: Life in its Truth: the Moment Present being more true in the Now; affirming that: existence is Real; a statement of Truth; and being in the Present Awareness; acknowledging existence, acknowledging and being totally aware that YOU ARE! The writings in the Books of "IS" are rhythmic and poetic, some symbolic and metaphoric in nature, while possibly being literal also. Rhythms in symbolic forms, (metaphors are like symbols) are capable of by-passing the brain's left hemisphere of reasoning and logic, allowing informational exchange to take place at a cellular level, enabling individuals, who choose to do so, to raise their light frequency-vibration rate. This, The Knowledge And Language Of The Light, The Language Of The Light "unlocked", is the Divine DNA. There are 64 codons (a sequence of three bases in a strain of DNA that provides the genetic code for a specific amino acid) in our genetic code. 44 of them are unused. Part of the RNA is also unused, (its as if its waiting for further instructions.) The RNA (ribonucleic acid) is The Messenger. It carries the code for specific amino acid sequences from the DNA to the cytoplasm for protein synthesis. Ribosomal RNA exists within the ribosome's DNA-passive "data storage device", comprising active material, carried in the form of bio-electromagnetic signals. These are photos-processing corpuscular and wave properties, perfectly capable of transmitting energy and information. An exaration of the bio-electromagnetic field is transmitted to the DNA. Through research and observation, their thoughts are that it seems people are changing at a molecular level, for it has been found that people have developed what appears to be a 3rd strain of DNA: Our DNA is changing...becoming more perfect! Our cells are "lightening up", regenerating, and perfecting! Our body, all that we are, is evolving into a higher frequency. One could call this: "awakening" to life and to all that we truly are, all that we are meant to be. We are remembering and re-membering all the true "You's" and "IS" together into one "US" of "We becoming I AM". We are remembering the first and the last that becomes ever the "circling-ever-source" of all existence: The Great Mystery, The Creator Force and Source, and All Of Creation.

It is my hope that the writings in this book and future books I write, "touch" you in such a way that you will experience the peace and love of connecting with your Spirit and Soul, and there-by "touching" The Great Divine. By doing this, it is my hope that you will access your own Innate Spiritual Gifts, and Messages, from The Divine and Spiritual Helpers, so that you might heal that which is needed healed, and re-member those parts of you that need re-membered, remembered, and need unity. By "re-membering" and remembering the Divine Connection to The Great Mystery, "God-Goddess", you then will be assisted by Divine Inter-Vention in the moving upwards in a Journey-Way Of Joy and Goodness; adjusting peacefully in Beauty, the Beauty-Way, the ascension into the Higher Light Of Becoming more of what we are and what we are all meant to become. This Planet Gaia, (Earth) and all upon her are in need of our Together-ness, our Unity, of Loving Mind and Light. She "sings" to us to "dance" our loving and peaceful "Soul-Heart" with feeling, into the "Heart" of All That she IS, and all that she creates, and all she was created for. All this includes the Elements, and Clan-doms: the Cells, Fungus, Microscopic Life, etc; the Minerals, the Insects, the Plants, the Animal and Human-Kind, etc.…All that comprises her : your mother of your human body : Earth! "Hold on to your Heart-Of-Heart's Dream", Dear Reader, for we are moving towards Singularity! We are moving into, and creating as we move the oneness of balance, peace, light and love; rejoining the sacred circle of life! Rejoining Love, for we ARE Love…

Stand Still, and Keep A Calm and Singular "EYE".

I hope my writings will "wrap" themselves around you in their loving intention, soothing you like lullabies, into yourself that is Divine and knows all that IS. I desire and wish for you to access your own DNA of The Blessed Memories, that shall guide you in survival, balance, wisdom, and love; bringing you into truth, understanding, and knowing, by way of their "Song" and your "Dance Of Contemplating", imagining (image-ing), and thinking and stilling; thereby, activating, both the left hemisphere of your brain, and, the right hemisphere: coming together into the Sacred "Marriage Of Singularity", thus, "dancing" out in beauty and ecstasy the truths of Creator's and life's goodness, love and purpose for you. It is crucial we travel back into our connective-ness of all that is Holy and Divine. The energy frequency upon Earth is resonating throughout all things… "calling" to us to return back home to the "Dance" Of Oneness" and becoming, and there-by gain our personal "Song" and join it again with the "One song". The Earth sings! She "dances"! The Stars "sing" and they "dance"! The sun and the moon and the universe "sings and dances"! UNI: one, unity, together-ness; VERSE: song, many, sound, communicating. Universe: the one and the many, united in song: Sound and Light, "Dancing"… Universe then means also the many of The One Song in unity… We are a melody of the God-

Goddess Song. Gaia is also singing The One Song, and she is singing it to us and to The Source-Of-All-Things. We are also a melody of her "song". Let us "sing" the song well! Let us "sing" our love into it, with the intent for the best for ALL creation. Let us lift it up to join The One Song Of "God". It is the way of things. It is The Beauty-Way. It is what and who we are. May you relax into this intended beauty and love of the writings, and if you desire it, allow them to draw out your own inner "stories", your own "songs", your Beauty "Song And Dance", to then add to not just this book, which is your own personal "dance" and "song" guide and journal, but add it to the many "songs" in The One Song Of Creation's Continuous United Beauty "Song And Dance". For indeed all that we do and say, and think and feel becomes... Let The Becoming be creations of joy and love, which serves good and beauty to and for all of us! We will then receive the knowledge, understanding, and wisdom we search for and need, if our hearts are with the intention of good for all. Your encoded memories that may awaken in you, by way of these writings, are assisted and "stirred" by light first, and for-most, from The Source Of All Sources: Our Creator. They will awaken only loving and spiritually good memories/understanding/knowledge and wisdom that was imprinted in us at the time of creation, of harmonious truths and survival. For these writings and their intentions are vibrations of love and light of a caring nature and intention from the higher realms for life's continuality. They are filled with the intention of love for all that is good and loving. They are of God-Goddess Light. They are of the Divine Feminine Principle Of God, the Shekinah's "Light And Sound" Of Love, that we are needing, especially NOW! These writings are Sacred Literature for your Spirit and your Soul. Your Soul is your Spirit connection with Eternity to the unveiling of your own Divinity, and the destiny of human kind. To connect with the Great Mystery, you need to get the mind's busy-ness out of the way of the Spirit and Soul, allowing Self to fill up with the Holy Great Spirit...Shekinah! One way of doing this is by the reading (seeing) and the hearing (listening) of Sacred Literature. (Sacred Literature stimulates the Soul and its connective-ness with The Divine---The Mysteries of God and Life). Activate the Soul connection and Shekinah Spirit first and then you can apply the Divine Mind to spiritually think and sense and know. Then contemplate, with imagination, and reasoning's probability, on what you receive or learn. The Spirit and Soul yearns to re-connect with The Divine. It will "tug" at you until it does. It is each Soul's choice whether to make that journey and channel Divinity, or withhold it. The Higher Purpose calling, is calling us to unite the ego with "God-Goddess" (Supreme Intelligence and Holy Spirit: The Shekinah) so it can bring about accomplishments of the "Heart of The Eternal Soul-Spirit".

HOW TO USE THIS BOOK:

* ***Please read*** *about the graphics and drawings in this book. That information can be found on page 161 in the back of this book. The drawings play a major part in the use and affect of this book.*

By reading the writings contained in this book, and then entering The "Silence", The Place Of Stillness Within, it is my hope, that you, the reader, shall then fill up with the 'Holy Ghost"/"Great Holy Spirit", The Shekinah; and in doing this, gain access to your Over-Soul and The Divine True Mysteries of Self, Life, and The Creator Source Of All Existence. It is my hope you then will gain well-being, joy, love, health, personal power, and therefore, all you require for a beautiful Being-ness existence. This then adds to the good results of Divinity, thus, to all people and all creation, all "worlds"; changing the worlds for the better, one "step" at a time, one breath, one movement, one heart beat at a "time". Know, there are many ways to enlightenment. Listed are some of these ways: metaphors, chants, dance, and rhythmic reading or/and listening to certain sounds, the sense of smell, and visual affects, (and using all of the 5 senses) induces the Mystical "Dance" of intimacy and ecstasy response...the filling up with the Holy Essence...Holy Spirit (Shekinah) and connecting with the Holy Intelligence. These manners of assisting "tools" stirs the Spirit and awakens the Soul with a kind of Sacred Song/Music, Light, and Spirit, allowing one to enter a deeper brain frequency, accessing a deeper reality and truth. The symbolic gestures and purpose of this, including self-examination, discipline, contemplation, archetypes; visualizations; prayer; and mantras, (visuals and sounds that awaken Spirit) transform The Self and the world around us. You will still face obstacles, test and trials, for these are the Universe's way of acknowledging you, saying you are Master of your own destiny, and gifting you "material" (things) to practice mastering, transforming and re-creating. It is the Universe's way of calling upon you to neutralize and harmonize---co-create with it, not against it. When these chaotic happenings presents themselves, sense your Divine Spirit and enter your Soul, feeling your empowerment, peace, and love.

"Keep a Calm and Clear Single Eye*".*

Face your fears of the "Storm" (the "shaking loose") feel at one with you Soul, and know: "Now this too shall pass", and know that your Soul connective-ness along with the knowing of your True Self's connection with the Divine, "shall set you free"...(out of bondage) Disharmonies/imbalances come to you because the Universal Supreme Mind/Intelligence, is trying to communicate to you what you were created for and who you truly are: a part of The Great Divine which is The-One-Source that is The Power-Over-All-Powers, God-Goddess; "The One" that is the Creator of the Universe and All That IS, Was, and Shall Ever Be. When you feel a Heightened Sense of your Soul, then The Divine Spirit has entered into your "Temple" (physical body). This is the way to know the difference from your imagination and the Soul's Truths speaking to you. You feel something beautiful and Loving pulling you. You feel something is about to happen and come forth, and you feel distracted from the mundane acutance around you. You then are being engaged into a "Mystery". This Mystery could be a trial, a test of faith, a message, or synchronicity of event that validates an Insight. The Divine manifests in challenges that bring one to understanding and knowledge. This brings one to Wisdom, thus Enlightenment. This then leads to: **That***, which we seek.* **That***, which we are and are ever* **Becoming...** *Mystical Experiences happen* **when one is ready for them***. "The Teacher" will come, (stimulating: rising the Teacher within), when the "student" is ready", is a popular saying. The Inner Teacher will rise up, spiraling and moving forward, when you, the "Seeker" truly seek with your "Heart" and not will The Ego alone nor The Intellect alone. When you seek, proclaiming in a voice of certainty and desire:* **"I am ready***!" then your Holy and Divine Spirit shall open the "Gates" to move upward and re-connect with your Divine Soul and The-Soul-of-Souls.*

Our Soul is like our Divine Song that God/Goddess hears and sings back to us. It is our "Eternal Heart", our "Eternal Fire". Become one with it. This I hope will transpire for you. This I hope to accomplish by making these writings and teachings available to you. This I was spiritually lead to do by the Creator Of All Things: (The God-Goddess Of First Creation), and guided by "Their" Spirit/Angel Messengers, Guides, and Masters in doing it. The purpose of these Books in connecting you with your Divine Soul is also so you can engage with it for processes/purposes of healing Self and the Planet, on ALL levels. With the engagement of the Spirit with the Soul, "they" will communicate to you instructions to get your body, mind and emotions back into harmony with your Spirit, Soul and Personality. This is the True "Marriage" every one seeks. This is the True Soul-Mate(ing). This will happen instantly if you are willing to listen with True "Heart"; acting on those instructions the instant you receive them. All this comes by "steps" so do not fret or stress to achieve these things quickly. They shall arrive in due time. Spiritual Truths and consecutiveness arrive by way of the peace and faith, and the intention of your desires. Be patient with your self, it shall bring you peace and thereby "open The Door" for that Soul connection with The Divine Soul of The Great Mystery. It will "dance" your "Inner Song" with song, and that song shall lift you to the Heavens and on to God-Goddess attunement. Enjoy your journey. Be at one with it, feeling its caress and beauty. Feel its song and dance. It is a song and dance of love. Love yourself and embrace all of you. It is the way to wholeness, truth and happiness. Build up your Spiritual Stamina with right actions and practices that enrich the Soul. Do not let challenges discourage you from your path, nor allow the illusions of the world and your mind's doubts pull you into deceptions and misperceptions. The Soul gradually awakens us to its relationship with the Divine; you will then detach from the earthy conscience and enter into the so-called Non-Reality (Dream) of your Soul-Conscience. Relax and let your own Divine Timing find you. Imagining, art, writing, music, singing, dancing, silence, nature, prayer and poetry are means of lifting you out of ego and body, withdrawing your conscience from the physical world of time and space, and into the Cosmic Soul-Song…

Music Of The Spheres: "The One Song"; "The Unity Song".

Read this book at a comfortable pace: your own pace. Do not struggle with understanding it. Just be. Relax and allow your Spirit to move with it, as you read this book or listen to the readings of The Books of "IS" audios. Let the writings "dance you into them". Let them dance inside you to bring about more of "The Becoming" of your Soul's connective-ness and Divinity. Then enjoy the re-reading of them. You will discover then that you may receive different insights at different readings. Those timings are your Divine Self's timings for insights, understanding and enlightenment. When you feel your Spirit and Soul moving and "calling to you", feeling a desire to write down or record, on tape, what is coming to you, do so. When this happens, allow it to flow forth from you with ease. It may come forth as poetry, metaphor, or simply as words running together. This is a process; and will all come together for you personally in time. This book is to be your own personal journal of Soul Records and communion with the boundless Divine inside you, and all around you. Look at the meditative, symbolic and Mandela-like (in nature), drawings of each chapter. Do they awaken any insights, memories, or In-Spirations? (I spelled inspirations this way to signify: In-Spirit. The words came forth while attuning to the Holy Spirit (Shekina) within, and the Higher Dimension Of Soul, and on up to The Great Creator-"Mystery"). Know and remember: ***you are special!*** *Everyone and everything* ***IS.*** *We* ***ALL*** *hold a "Piece of The Great Mystery". We all are to remember this and* ***re****-member "The Main Pieces of The truth" of these Sacred "Mysteries". Everyone has all the "pieces", yet no one person here in this dimension has all The Conscious-Awareness-Memories of the "Pieces". We are one "body" caught in the belief/illusion that we are all separate from one another, our Creator and all life. Lets assist one another in the remembering so we can* ***re****-member the "parts of the whole body" of this Creation (Creator) that created us, and all things, back "together". Together let us* ***re****-member these "pieces" back (together)," mending The Sacred Hoop".*

SUGGESTION: MEDITATION

*** Before you begin reading this book or listening to it on audio, try this:**

"Find a place to sit, (Or lie or sit, if you are listening to this on audio) where it is quiet and you will not be disturbed for the time you plan on journeying. Next, get comfortable, loosening any clothing that causes you distraction or discomfort. Take several deep breathes through your nose and exhale through your mouth, expelling all stagnated air, allowing your abdomen to rise with each inhale and lower with each exhale. Refresh! Relax and close your eyes for the moments it takes for you to feel you have made contact with your Soul. When you feel that touch of oneness, again take a deep joyful

breath and exhale with love and gratitude. Rejoice in the feeling of it! Smile. Smile with joy and love to your insides and all the Inner Universe of cells and microcosmic life there that makes up there: ***YOU and Your Inner Universe Of "stars" And Life!*** *Now smile with that same perfect love and joy to all that is around you, where you are now. Next, move your feelings and that visualization out to cover what is beyond that, continuing on in Circles Of Love to in-circumference the entire planet; moving out ward still to the many multi-levels of worlds, and on into infinity with the Source-God-Goddess of First Cause, and First Conscience. Here you take another deeper breath and bathe in its Love Light Of Perfection. Notice any sensations there. Notice any around you and inside you. Notice your beating heart, the Sacred "Drum". Now listen with it for your Soul-Song. Can you "hear" it? Then, sing it! Do not be shy. Do not try to think. Just be, and let your song become. Open your mouth without any thoughts of what will come forth. Just let it arrive and spring forth in sound. When you do, feel it image. Bring in all of the five senses and notice them in this song. Allow them to move into the sixth sense. If you feel like dancing, get up and dance! Move your arms, hands, fingers, head, legs, feet, eyes, tongue, and body. Stir up the Spirit! Let it rise to meet with The Over-Soul, and the Super-Conscience! Let them be "Dance Partners"! See them swirl and gesture in symbols! Join the movements in your Sacred Mind's-Eye and see and feel and enact the "Dance" they are dancing…* ***you*** *are dancing! Sing your Soul-Song! Sing the Songs of Life! Sing the Song of anything you wish to know, but let it be of good intent, for the good of all, harming none. Sing: "only good comes from me, only good comes to me! I am love, I am joy, I am harmony, I am abundance, and I sing and dance my Eternal Divinity! It is good and so it is so!" Laugh out loud with joy! Fill up with ecstasy! Know you are loved and more of Love then one can comprehend at this "marked-period" of consciousness on Earth! So vast, so plentiful and so beautiful is The Truth of all that we are, and all that* ***IS****! When you feel filled with The Holy Spirit/Great Spirit/ Great Mystery, and feel your Soul has risen to touch that Divine-ness; then breathe again and relax with it back inside your Self, and your physical body of matter. Hum your song and Sway-Dance gently with it. When you instinctively feel you should open your eyes, do so slowly* ***keeping*** *the feelings and connective-ness you have created and received. Now, begin reading this book, or if you are listening to this on audio, pause it until you feel the peace and love connection within you, then press play and enjoy! Listen with your Heart-Spirit, The Heart-Of-Hearts, with your Higher Soul, and with the consciousness of where you just were and now are.*

Breathe!

May this book bring the love and good intentions it was created to bring to you, the world, and the many worlds within worlds that make up all creation: the Creator! May you "awaken" from this "Dream", this illusion, of "darkened" falsehood and fear, and gain the Memories of how it is meant to be and who you are: Children Of Light, Children Of "God! We have been "lost" in a "Dream", "asleep", for a long "time". Let us NOW "wake up"! It is "time"! Let us "Dream" The World we were meant to "Dream" (Create), TOGETHER, as a connected Sacred-Double-Hoop, a Sacred Family. Many as ONE, with the All Mighty Creator! "Dream" on, Dear Reader, in this Sacred "Dream-Time". Be a "Dreamer, yes, but, be a WISE "Dreamer" of Truth!

"I wish for you health, beauty, and enlightenment. I wish for you The Truth that is you: A Divine-All-Knowing-Spirit-Of-Light-And-Love, having a human experience. I wish for you love, knowledge, understanding and the wisdom to know The Truth; and I wish you the awareness of the Special Relationship you have with the Loving Higher Power, The Creating Force. I wish you to know your important part and meaning in this Universe. I wish for you the Eternal-"YOUR-Song" so that you might feel the beauty and The Love along with The Truth and the stories lying in rhythm within you, and so know the One-Song of all Beauty of all existence, and then again in Harmonic Union join your Song with it. I wish for you to feel and know The Truths of Creation, life and you; and the story and the many "stories", seeming there at times, and camouflaged at others, "dancing out" to you and caressing you with what they gift in awakening your innate knowing of Divine love, knowledge, wisdom, understanding and truth. I wish for you The "Dance" of the activation of your Light's Higher Domain; assisting you in The Ascension Of Your Conscious, your body and this planet; bringing you also into The "Song" Of Understanding And Empathy With Life, so it will always keep you aware and instinctive for all the best of you and the best for you. I wish you that "Song" and I wish you...

"This Dance of Becoming"

Enjoy The Journey into 'The Dance of Becoming'
"The Journey with Spirit into the Within of your Soul"...

Lovingly,
The Author,
Dr. R. Lowery-Hawk

Post Note: *Due to DR. R. Lowery-Hawk's many years of challenges/ "teachings" with and about her health/healing; plus all the other challenges and "set- backs" that came with it, it has taken ten extra years longer then she had originally planned on publishing this first book: The BOOKS OF "IS". The writings in this book cover a twenty-eight-year span. Dr. R. Lowery-Hawk kept her faith in what she was being Spiritually lead and "instructed" to do by the Supreme Creator, Higher Dimensions, The Galactic Federation, Creator's Angelic assistants, (and those others dwelling in the Most High places) She knew The BOOKS OF "IS": Book One, would be published; and, published under Divine Intervention and Divine Synchronicity, but "The Books" would be published when they were meant to be, **when others were more of a need and desire for them**. The Creator God/Goddess, Supreme Intelligence's "Christ Energy of Love", sent out an "Urgent-like-Call" to the Author to NOW have the first Books Of "IS" published; and later, according to which way human kind creates the happenings here in their "Dream-time", have the other Books of "IS" published, plus, the other books, (going by other titles), and messages, she has written, available for others to hear and to read. Others, besides the Author, have been Spiritually receiving, in the mission of good, similar Messages, and are also feeling, and hearing the urgent call to "come forth"–telling them: "the time is NOW!" That "Call" is telling them that these Messages of Truth need to come forth again at this time, and be delivered for the welfare of the planet, for human-kind, for all life on the planet, and all life that is **beyond, and, beyond the beyond**, of what most do not realize---(**yet**), is affected by us and this planet, as they too, affect us. The Author is happy and grateful to be able to now, after all these years, present this first Book of "IS": **"The Dance of Becoming"** to you and to others, for the intention of Good and Love for us all, in The-Sacred-Circle-Of-Life!*

May these writings bless you and open to you!

WELCOME TO THE BOOKS OF:

* *Dr. R. Lowery-Hawk is continuing to focus upon greater future complete health for herself and the planet as a whole.*

** For more about the Author, See:*
"Bio on the Author", located in back of book pg. 165
And Book Preview about the Author, pg. 180

✡ ✡

The Books of "IS"

Book One:

"The Dance of Becoming

*The first in a series of thought provoking books, having the intention of delivering Messages of Quantum Wisdom and Knowledge/ Ancient Truths for Spiritual Enlightenment/Ascension and Well Being. The writings herein are **"Seeds"** of a philosophic and Mystical nature. Many are from our Star Relations and the Celestial Hierarchy, all from & assisting the Great Mystery God Light. These are Messages of rhythmic, Mystical, and metaphorical contemplations of a Shamanic nature: Mysticism, Insight, Wisdom, poetry; "myth" and story; with contemplative and meditative drawings, affirmations, Inspirations, and various other Spiritual Writings; all moving towards:*

Knowledge, Understanding, Wisdom, and Enlightenment of:

"THE KNOWING"

The Books of "IS"

Are a series of books to also assist you in:

The Awakening of the Soul Conscience

* The Ancient Truth-Mysteries *

The Journey into your Soul

The Spirit-Child Within

The Super Conscience

All GEARED TOWARDS:

UNLOCKING THE SACRED AND DIVINE MEMORIES ENCODED IN THE DNA: THE SOUL'S RECORDS FOR ESSENTIAL WELL BEING AND INTENTION; FOR KNOWLEDGE AND HIGHER PURPOSES FOR THE SELF, OTHERS, THE PLANET, AND, FOR THE "SURVIVAL OF THE TIMES".

* Written and Illustrated by the Author

* Book Design by the Author

"Although there are a great number of (spiritual) practices, all of them have a common purpose because all of them are methods for subduing our controlled mind. Our present mind is like a wild elephant----out of control and hard to tame."

---------- Geshe Kelsang Gyaatso,

"IS"

I **S**ense

Inner **S**elf

Inner **S**pirit

Inters **S**ource

Inner **S**ight

Internal **S**ight

Immortal **S**oul

Infinite **S**ource

Inters: **S**hekinah,

Inner Shekinah

***

I SHALL *BE*

FOR, ***I AM...***

ALL OF

EVERYTHING

IS

So

That

SHhhhE - H-ISssss

Webster's Dictionary...IS:

1. Present tense of ***be;*** 2. Third person ***singular***

ISIS

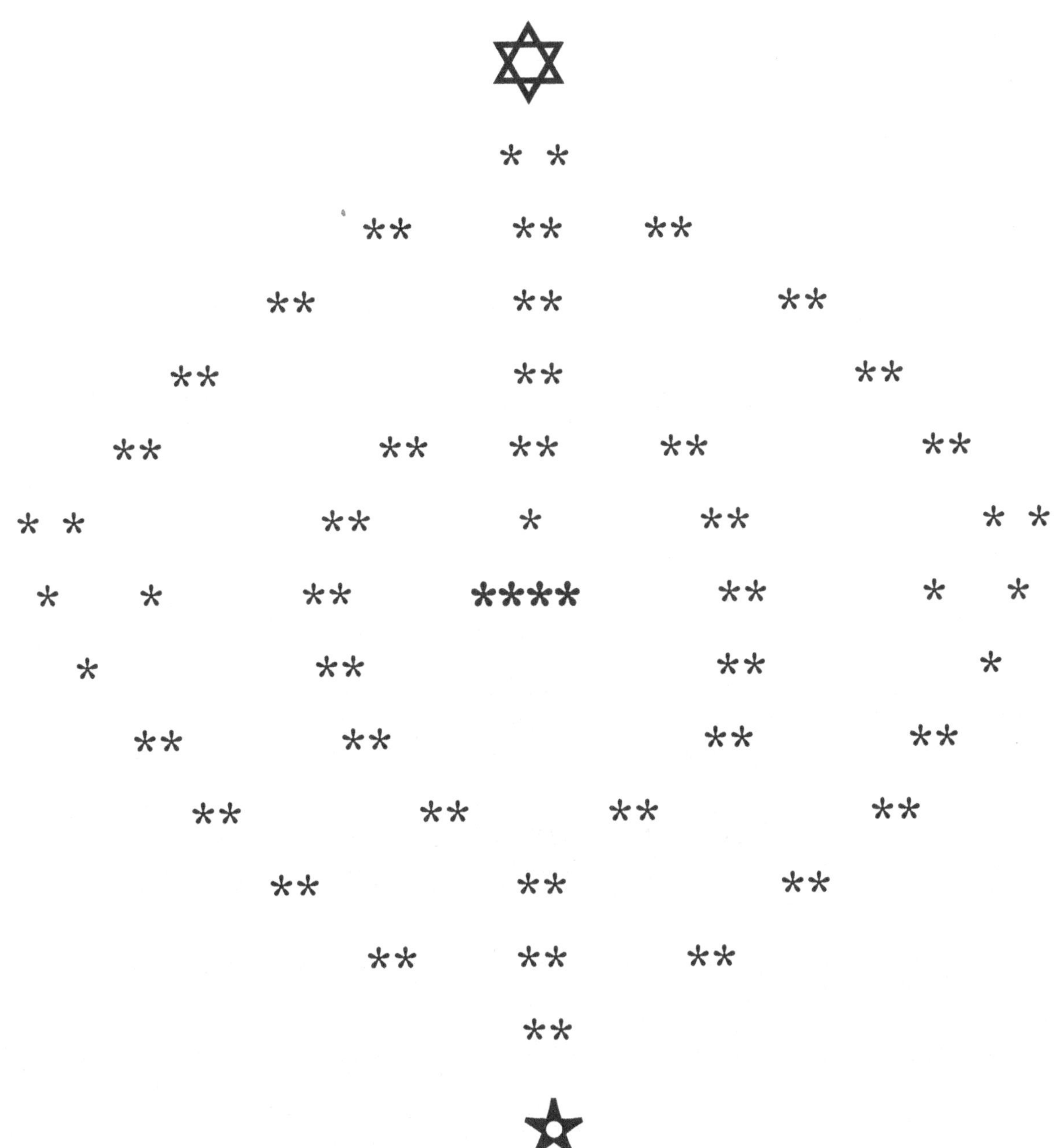

"ALIGNING THE STARS"

ABOVE AND WITHIN

THESE WORDS HEREIN ARE:

For those who seek the Light in earnest,
to know the Light, and be of the Light;
so to bring forth the Light:
In Truth and Love.

____The Author,
Wednesday, February 16, 2012

The Universe surrounds me

I wonder in it where I be?
I see the mountains, the valleys,
And the life within the sea.

I travel life's uncertain paths,
They bellow out to me...
And I, forever wandering on the path, ask:
"Where in this universe is me?"

Could I be the grass so green?
Perhaps, the sky so blue?
Or, do I go beyond these bounds,
Even far beyond the "Sea"?

Do I shrink and do I swell;
Or do I stay then cease to be?
...But then... could that far away, above,
Be far beyond what my eyes can see?

Could it be an outer-look,
Of What is also inside of me?
Am I then what it may be;
And, is it then what be me?

*...IF this all **IS** the Universe,*
And, it all is unknown to me,
Where then do I fit in?
Am I lost in this Great Cosmic Sea?

The Universe surrounds me,
Forever drifting in it,
Lost I might seem...
YET,

Somewhere deep within myself,
I somehow know...
I am a part of:
This Great Cosmic Dream...

"This Great Cosmic Dream"

Written: November 19, 2002, 1:15 A.M.

✡

* * *** Once upon a time…*** * *

* ** There was Black and White Darkness ** *

And it was this way for ALL *eternity…*

* * * **Then man and woman were made…** * * *

* * * + * * *

And a King came,

And told the other Kings

To send out their Most BRAVEST *Warriors:*

The Moon and The Sun,

** **

To fight the Black Darkness,

And, the White Darkness…

Then a brave Sun came and

fought the Black Darkness

++++ *The Sun* only fought the Black Dark*ness* *++++*

Then the Moon came,

And fought the White Darkness.

Then, the world was clear again…

…But God came

And told the "King" he was going to make

Animals and other people.

"THE END"

"God's Decision"

**** *MORAL OF STORY:* ****

"There is a God, and, it's a challenge to see if man
Could take care of him self and survive on Earth"

*** Story and moral, word for word, by my Granddaughter:**

Fantashia W.M.S. Whittington

(Age: 7 years old)

** Written and told to me by her ,on Sunday, August 5, 2001, 10:40 A.M.*

* * * * * * *

THE GREAT MYSTERY AND AUTHOR COMMUNICATING
(Second Intro)

Author: *"Are there stories to be told?"*

The Great Mystery/God/Goddess): "They are locked within each. 'Knock' and you shall know. Relax into knowing by way of contemplation, and your memories shall unlock before you."

Author: "You have communed with me for many years, and I have written down much of what you have made known to me. Am I clear that you are guiding me to make these writings available for others to read?"

The Great Mystery/God/Goddess): "Yes, this is still true. I have not changed my intent from that time you called the year 1984, when you had first become *certain* it was *I* who stirred you. You had touched your sorrow, deeply, and that 'cleared' the way for you to be aware of my messages. My messages then, at that time, were: that which was 'hidden' was but merely 'covered' by one's own busy-ness. Truth of all creation has always been revealed to the aware; but due to the many distractions that mankind himself/herself have created in their impatience to know; to experience; and to have; they ended up 'blinding' them- selves to that which was meant to be known; that which was *always* theirs. Mankind's many distractions have caused the truths to shrink back in camouflage, appearing hidden or lost. I, at that time, in the Earth year many refer to as: 1984, also revealed to you, that the fairy tales of your youth, which many children have also heard; the nursery rhymes and the songs sung; held truths in rhythm, yet seeming not there; fun and joyful, yet wise and assisting.

Humans have gotten caught up with a 'stranger', and that "stranger" moves them too quickly pass the path, liken unto the Tiger Beetle. The Tiger Beetle I created to move at a tremendous speed. It moves so quickly it cannot see until it pauses and focuses. I created the Tiger Beetle to move quickly for its survival, but I did *not* create man to rush so fast, for I created man, to slow down a part of *myself*. This is for creation, and for the *survival* of creation. This slowing down parts of me was so that I might *observe* myself by way of 'pausing'. This pausing is not fully in your awareness, but for my ever-changing much higher frequencies, mankind's experiences are like pauses for me: moments to reflex upon myself. Mankind and all life are reflexions of my thoughts and movements. All creation is then a replica of *me*, and so, must have their 'pauses' to reflex, observe, ***and,***

Become!

...Therefore, *TIME* was given...

'SLOW DOWN SO THAT YOU MIGHT KNOW!'

Your writing down what comes through you, by way of me, and then your reading and contemplating what you have written down, is one form of slowing down---pausing, so that you might know, and become more of *that* which you came from! This is why... I pause... In the year you called 1984, I had made known to you that many books and many movies going under the titles of: science fiction; fantasy; myth; fairy tales; stories; poetry; metaphors; and other seemly imaginative works, held truths within them, by their creators, who were consciously aware; and, by those, creating these truths forms, who were *not fully* aware, on a conscience level, of their creations. Their work, their creation, was made possible so that others could also 'see' and/or read the truths, and thus, 'awaken' back to themselves and, their origin. These supple truths are 'seeds'. You, too, have been called to put into print that which has, and is, awakening to you. It is as I had said then: 'These are 'seeds', given, so that they might be 'nourished' and then grow strong; give, so to 'bear their fruit'. Before the fruit there is always the flower. That 'flower' is the soul's memories that are encoded and stored in the DNA: stored inside of *each* living creation in the Universe! Each life form of various kinds have I encoded with records of *all* existence; of all that I AM! This, you call DNA; and some call: the Akashic Records; while others refer to this as: 'The Book of Life'. You, (everyone and everything) carry within you then, not only the 'Flower of Life', but also the 'Book of Life'...*my 'DNA'*! You carry this, *because you* **are** *this*! You are an *extension* of me! You are *ALL* 'Star Lights', Children of The Light, from the Light: **that** which **I AM**! I AM the Light, and the Light ***IS*** the Way... The 'Fruit' that I spoke of, that comes after the 'Flower', is the return of the rhythm of my Soul's Memories. Not only the return *to* the Memories, but to the *rhythm* of *what* they awaken in you, of the Truths, of *what* you are, and *how* you are to *maintain* the ***True Essence*** of **What and *Who*** you are: how to "dance with the stream" of life's 'Song'. The 'Song' propels you *towards* life, and the 'Dance' is *how* you get there. *Where* you are going is towards **your *Be-coming*.** You are becoming *more* then you are now. Many eons from now when you will have achieved 'God-head-like' status, you too, will cast forth 'New Worlds' that will strive to become more then what they were in the beginning. You then will become a Great Mystery to them. I have told you, that the way my messages and my memories are to awaken the "God-Seeds", lying dormant in the

DNA, is by way of *voice* from one to another; yet, because human kind has increased in numbers quickly, upon the planet, influencing greatly, the 'dream' *all* of you are 'dreaming', (Yes, "dreaming", even while you yet "sleep"), there is now then, an urgency to restore memory and thus, balance, to massive numbers of people at the same time. The best way to accomplish this, at this time, is by way of the media. This I speak of includes: books; newsletters; television; movies; radio; cartoons; tapes; CDs; computers; group speaking; seminars; work shops; retreats; and the like... Yes, Child of Light, **I AM** leading you: calling to you, inspiring you, to move forward and to write and write, ***and, write***; to put into print; to speak to others of these things, as I lead you *to, and,* to **whom** I lead you to do so! Speak these messages, and these memories, before others in groups, so that others will feel their own memories stir to 'break forth' and free of their dormant 'Seeds' that they have settled back into. Speak and write also, so that those like yourself, who have agreed to awaken now, might share the energy and the memories of one another, for *that* shall enable all of you to nourish the 'Seeds' so that they will 'spring forth' naturally into full purpose. In doing this, you shall draw down, and, draw forth,

The-'Forgotten-Time'...

I have said, that I wish for you to write down and to speak, at times in: metaphor, poetry, songs, stories, and myths. I have guided you this way because they are calming and rhythmic. Rhythm creates rhythms. Rhythms creates dance. They are movement. Both, pattern themselves after the breath. All of life is breathing, for life ***IS***! The universe is breathing! *All* life is alive, and breathes me in! This breathing draws **all** life back to me: "**The First Cause**"; **the First Breath**; and then, back to my individualized, yet extended expressions, of me: ALL of creation! We: **you**; ALL life; *unites* with *each inhale*; and we share *each* of our experiences and our being, each time we *exhale*. In doing so, we are reminded that we are ONE, one *being* with *many* parts, functioning, for the *whole*! ***Your*** memories, then, are ***MY*** memories; ***MY*** memories then, are ***YOURS***. And, so it is: I speak to you many times in rhythm, in the breath of song and dance, in poetry, metaphor, song, and story. Your brain's neurons, and your DNA, easier receives rhythms, such as these. That is *one* of the reasons for the parables in the times of Jesus' teachings. The other reason for the parables; the metaphors; psalms; and myths; are so that each person may discover the truths, therein: the seemingly hidden meanings, at the time that one's individual free will *accepts* the *readiness* of their Soul to *consciously* 'awake' and move forth, in ***remembrance of me***! The poetic stories and verses then, are to 'rock you back to me', **back,** into: **memory**! Mankind is in the 'Season-Of-The-Era' of the **Sacred Union**:

the '**Sacred Marriage**'! This that I speak of is **'the coming together of the Mother-Father God!'** I AM *all* life, and so then, I AM also, '*The Mother*' Over the ages, man has separated the 'Mother from the Father'. Man has separated the ***Image and the Likeness*** of what I represent. Therefore, they have 'lost understanding'. I am both sources of life: male and female: counter-parts, seen in all that make up existence as you know it. My 'call' is a call back to 'The Sacred Union'. This means male and female are to 'Embrace in their Sacredness'. It is *this* that is balance! It is *this* that is the feeling of completeness! 'The Mother' is 'pregnant' and about to give 'birth', and *all of you* are to be her '**mid-wives**'! I AM calling '**my Female Essence back home**', and, I AM 'calling 'her' to '**embrace the Male Essence**', while I 'call' the 'male', ***to 'embrace her' Essence***'. It is 'needed' *if* 'mankind' (human-kind) is to continue in the 'Dance of Creation'. If one is to ***truly*** know *me*, that one ***must*** be *willing* to ***embrace ALL of me***! In doing so, know then, that

I AM also Earth Mother!

I AM all you can see, and all that you think you cannot see; all you can feel and touch; smell; sense; and taste; and all that you think you cannot... I AM all that you breathe, know, and think. Know, I AM 'man', but know that I AM 'woman' also! I AM ALL THAT I can be. I AM THAT... I AM That I AM, so That, I AM...

I AM *more* than I seem...

'I AM...*the Great Mystery!*'

Come,

"Dance with Me!"

WHAT ONCE WAS "IS"
"Message from: The Great Mystery-Creator
Written down by: Author, R.M. Lowery-S.F.E.-Hawk
December 2002

"The universe is made up of stories, *not* atoms."

----------- Muniel Rukeyser

"LIFE IS A CIRCLING STORY"

----The Author
February, 14, 2011

(A story of the deeper self...)

"TURN OVER A LEAF..."

"WHAT DO YOU SEE?"

The Author
Heard and shown in dream
in Winter 1990
Written July 11, 2011

* *

An inquiry into what is false and true
of existence in general...
Must be carried by constant practice
throughout a long period...
At last in a flash, understanding of
each blazes up, and the mind,
as it exerts all its power to limit of
human capacity, is flooded with light.

----Plato

UNDERSTANDING

brings the Light. The Light brings "The Golden Keys" for the opening of the "Golden Gates" to your "awakening in the Dream", and moving beyond the beyond.

----The Author, Dr. R. Lowery-Hawk
Monday, February 21, 2011

WHEN YOU ARE READY,
THE "TEACHER" SHALL
COME FORTH...

THAT TEACHER IS:
THE DIVINE SPIRIT WITHIN.

—The Author, Dr. R. Lowery-Hawk
February 19, 2011

"SEEK AND YE SHALL FIND..."

"KNOCK AND THE DOOR SHALL OPEN"

---Jesus, from the Christian Bible

"THE DOOR IS OPEN..."

TO THAT WHICH WE SEEK:

GOING

BEYOND NOW,

BEYOND TIME,

BEYOND THE BEYOND...

"KNOW THY SELF"

---SOCRATES

CHAPTER ONE

"THE 'KEYS' TO THE HEAVENS"...

(The Time Lords' "Golden Keys")

**

"Awaken, Dear and Beloved Child,
In the dream you are dreaming."

----The Author, Dr. R. Lowery-Hawk

"The twilight of my heart dims...

What am I

But a minute piece of existence,
Waiting; pondering; motionless; drifting;
Standing elevated in void less space...?
If there is a time put upon existence,

What am I?

So tiny; so insignificant; so unnoticed by the billion grains of sands,
That makes up our lives?
If time stood still, and existence moved on,
Who's to say we stand as statues,
Or we tumble as weeds gone amuck?
"Here I sit",
On the edge of eternity
And ***still***, I swell as ignorant...
Given to me knowledge, existence, being,
All the wonders of AM,
Still,
I sit ,
Pondering, drifting,
Making, (more or less),
Nothing out of **my time**,
nothing out of ***me***...
Given a chance,
Would I fling it all back into the face of wonder?
Or,
Would I twist it, turn it?
Exam it ?
And hold tight my new,
yet **always there:**

"Given Treasure?"

"The Call"
Written: 1985

TIME WAS GIVEN AS A GIFT…

A LINE: ONE POINT TO ANOTHER;
A PATH TO TRAVEL:
MARKED OFF BY MEASURE,

TO OFFER YOU A BACKGROUND,
TO CO-CREATE AND GROW;

A PLAYGROUND:
A PLACE TO PLAY;

A PLACE OF STILLNESS:
TO BE YOU IN,
TO BECOME *ALL* IN:

TO BECOME…

THAT*:*
THE DIVINE YOU TRULY ARE,
THAT YOU ARE TRULY FROM…

I AM ***IS,***
THEREFORE,

I AM
YOU ARE,

ALL ***IS***

"The Gift Of Time"
Written: 1985

"VOICES OF THE ANCESTORS"

("The Ancient Grandmothers Speak")

ANCESTORS: ***"Our 'blood' and our 'bones' are here with Mother Earth.***

WE are here!

Part of what we are - our Spirit/Essence *is here*. Our flesh was returned to Earth Mother, and so, we are part of her. Our Spirits are here, yet our Spirits are also *beyond* most understanding. They are where one could call: Stars, or Spirit World, yet, a part of *all* that *IS*. The 'part' that is here, *needs* that 'part' of us that is *there* with you on Earth...

You must give us 'breath'! Your breath is life"!

'Breathe for us!'

Bring us to 'life' so that we can connect with our Souls in the Spirit World! Your breath will give life to your cells...the 'Seeds' of our children, our seven generations, before, to give life to the seven generations, after, that will give life, to the generations before that, and *beyond* THAT!'

RUBY: ***"What can we do for you?***

ANCESTORS: "Breathe for us! Light *your* 'Fires!' The 'Fires' (Internal 'Fires' and outdoor fires) will spark our life! Have *more* council fires, ceremony, and gatherings ***with*** the fire! We are the Ancestors of Truth and Balance -The Beauty Way!

WE assist, in the 'Dance'...

Your hair is worn loose to send prayers. The wind blows through it, and the wind gives them life, carrying the messages: your prayers, to us, to Mother Earth, the stars; and on to the Great Mystery! Your hair, it is like the grass and the trees that the wind stimulates to give life and growth! The hair braid contains the essence of the prayers, holding them, to gain, and contain, power! It is the symbol of the three-fold world: the coming together, (balance) of the gathering of physical-third-dimension-world. Mind, *must* be disciplined! Thoughts and emotions *must* be acknowledged and known; they *must* be disciplined! Body, *must* be fine tuned, purified and controlled...disciplined! Add to this, The Spirit, after they, the three parts, have bonded, and been mated and controlled together, as one, (as in the braid), held in power until calmed and disciplined; then let loose and free. This then, is Spirit, the forth addition to sending the prayers. The wind catches the braided prayers: the prayer braid bundle; and releases them in love, to the winds of change, and on to: the Great Creator"!

Walk softly upon us...!

Mother Earth, you walk upon, and so do you, *us*. Walk *gently* Children, for we 'feel' your Spirit through your feet. This you 'feed' to us, so you 'feed Mother', and so, the Creator also... and what you 'feed', you create! Your thoughts; your emotions; move through the body and create: Spirit! 'The Spirit-Wind'! You *are* the 'wind'! You are, the 'Spirit-Wind'! This you do not remember; but you *are* The Life! You are truly then, our 'blood', our life force. You then become a 'Creator', as you create a 'something' that goes out to the *Great* Creator and *attaches* to this Creator. (Yes, as you have spoken of: Attaching Spirits - so do you attach your *Spirit* to the Creator.) Your Spirit, as does ours, attaches to *ALL* forms, and is liken unto energy cells. So as you can 'see', each *is* the Creator, the Creating 'force' itself! Each life force stems from the *Great* Creator, comes forth from, and attaches to, returning *back*. Is your 'God/Goddess' cruel? Then look into your *own* 'looking-glass'! For you are *also, this* Creator, *this* creation. If you say: 'But I have *always* lived a Good Soul!' Then know, that other Souls are your Soul *also*. Give off then, your intended *Good Soul* to the crest and the core of the 'Heart Beat'. Give forth Prayer; Ceremony: loving thoughts & action, for 'blood' (Soul Essence), goes throughout *all* of the body (creation; Creator), and recycles full circle; and so, you see, you *add* to the 'blood': 'diseased blood' or 'pure blood'! *YOU* CHOOSE! This then is the *true* meaning of the word: 'pure blood' -'red blood', 'red road.' The breath 'feeds' the blood; keeps the cells alive; and so, *keeps* peace and purity *alive*; creating harmony; balance and Love.

'BREATHE US'!

"***Breathe us***, up and up and up! ***'Breathe us'!'*** Breathe us down and down and down! Let us rejoin our essence we left behind to 'feed' *you'*, to *hold* our memories. The Earth *holds* our 'Memories'. We gave our Memories... All who have lived before, (be their skin 'color' 'red/black/yellow/brown or white'), *ALL* have 'The Memories' - '*Collective* Memories'! These are calling to you! The 'Voices' of the 'Children' of long ago...of once before...' 'The Voices of the Ancestors'! Mother Earth then, is 'speaking' *through us*; we, *through her*, and then, *through you*. This is *why* many are 'returning', to The-Ways-Of-Truth-Of-Creation, and to Mother Earth's 'care-givers'. Connect with us *regularly* to keep the 'Memories alive'! These 'Memories' are 'Seed-Cells' that help renew 'dead ones', and so, keep the Earth 'alive'. Each thought of Light and Truth, renews a 'darken cell', and so gives, life, to a stored 'Record Keeper': stored encoded knowledge/wisdom/truths, the ebb and flow - life's pulsations, to maintain these life forms, on this planet. Your songs and your dances are life pulses - heart flow - life force energy - a 'stream'; a 'river' that 'washes clean' the 'Spheres of the Hemispheres' inside (you and the earth). Be the pure, 'clean hollow tube' - the 'hollow bone', so that the 'river' can move freely through you, to Earth Mother, to us; to life - *all* creation; and back to the 'Heart-Core'--- that which many think of as: 'God-Face'; 'Goddess-Force'-Source-Creator; and similar names. The fingernails are the hoods over sensitivity, and so, a message-reminder that your sensory system *also* must be guarded and shielded. As you grow, so must you harvest discipline, to serve as a 'hood', to buffer and to balance your gaining sensitive sensory-system. As 'time' is being 'removed' and new dimensions being birth, so then will your systems become fine tuned, high vibrating, and sensitive. Therefore, cultivate a 'hooded shield' that is in harmony with your growth, so as *not* to block, but rather, buffer; that you may *continue* to 'grow' more dimensionally..."

"*We have spoken*"...

"May Peace and Truth go with you."

"Received from the Grandmothers--The Ancestor's Spirits of long ago."
March 1994

WE ARE PART OF

THAT
CREATION
WHICH SEEKS
TO UNDERSTAND
All
CREATION!

WRITTEN: 2002

In the beginning, there was "*TIME*"...

Yet, not measured on a scale, nor by an action, but rather...

By The "Heart"...

Time was but an "invisible line", seen and not seen, depending upon one's own conception and perception of life. When the "heart" became "divided", duality came into a more "solid" form, changing into: a time measured, divided, and separated: Truth "cut into"; Spirit locked in substance; seen, felt, and believed to be...

"Substance believed into Being"...

This then became ONE agreed upon, substance, crystallized into a 3rd Dimensional World, referred to as: Matter! There came a "time" when the people began to once again feel the pulsating of the "heart" in the Earth beneath them. They began to also feel the pulsating of the "heart" above them, in the Heavens. Connecting these two "Hearts" with their own heart and then with those around them began their movement out of time and formed density, becoming more fluid and flowing; becoming a vapor of "mist"; substance moving, becoming... Substance moving from the solid-state, turns into: vapor, thus, "Time" removed... With this "removal" of "Time", there then came Spirit and Freedom. Duality, Time and Substance "belongs" to those who seek teachings on "planets". It is the taking in of "some-thing" of a denser vibration to weight the lightness of Spirit, so as to observe *slowly*, that which is to be "tapped". Duality is so to see *both* sides to things. It's to understand the *"difference"* of things, and to see which choice is the *better* one for *every* living thing. Substance allows us to feel, and imagine. We then observe and choose. We experience and learn. We seek to know and to understand much, and in the process, we learn how to be Creators of balanced Love and Harmony in the *Likeness* and *Image* of our Creator. Time is substance, creating illusions of duality and separation. When we then seek rest for a "time", OR, *FROM* "time", we then "step out and forth"; lifting up from time, substance, and bondage...

"REMOVE TIME" *And...*

YOU ENTER THE RHEALM

OF:

SPIRIT!

"Time, substance and Spirit"

WRITTEN 1999

There were two old men...

One born blind,

The other born with the sharp eye of the Eagle...

THE FIRST WAS MADE *TO* SEE,
THE SECOND WAS MADE TO *NOT* SEE...
The **first**, was the man born blind
Of the physical world;
But **the second**,
Whose eyes could see the smallest
Of smallest particles of dust,
And could describe in detail,
The ship that was the further away on the horizon,
Here, in the physical world,
Was 'blind' to the Spiritual World...
...And so, that the *1st blind man* might see
"The Great Challenger":
The illusions of the physical world,
In order that he might gain more "Sight",
He was given the gift of ***physical sight***...
...And, *the second man*,
Was ***made "blind"*** to the physical world
So that he might gain "Sight" of that which *lives*;
That he might gain "Sight" of that which "*Speaks*"
In The *Silence*, in The World *Beyond*

" The Illusion"...

"TO GAIN MORE SIGHT"
Written: 1994

✱

Every Flower
Has it's time under the Sun.
It must be allowed to Bloom...

****

Each Fruit Tree must be
Given it's time and season to
Bear fruit...

* *

****

"DO NOT THINK WITH THE MND OF THE COMMON MAN."

Relax and feel.
Allow your 'vision-inner-eye' to 'see'
The Truths I reveal,
And the added Truths
Your Soul then shall pour forth to you,
Like a spring of fresh water..."

✡

Message from:
"The Great Mystery"
1994

There are "strings" that are time numbered and coded; and numbers beyond time that string together the codes that form the "keys". The "keys" are a mystery to those who limit their thinking and their creativity; but therein lies the "Secret to the Heavenly "Gates"...

"The Secret sleeps as a Memory"...

THE AUTHOR
August 02, 2011
1:00 A.M. Tuesday

READER'S OWN IN-SPIRED WRITINGS

****

READER'S OWN IN-SPIRED WRITINGS

****

CHAPTER TWO

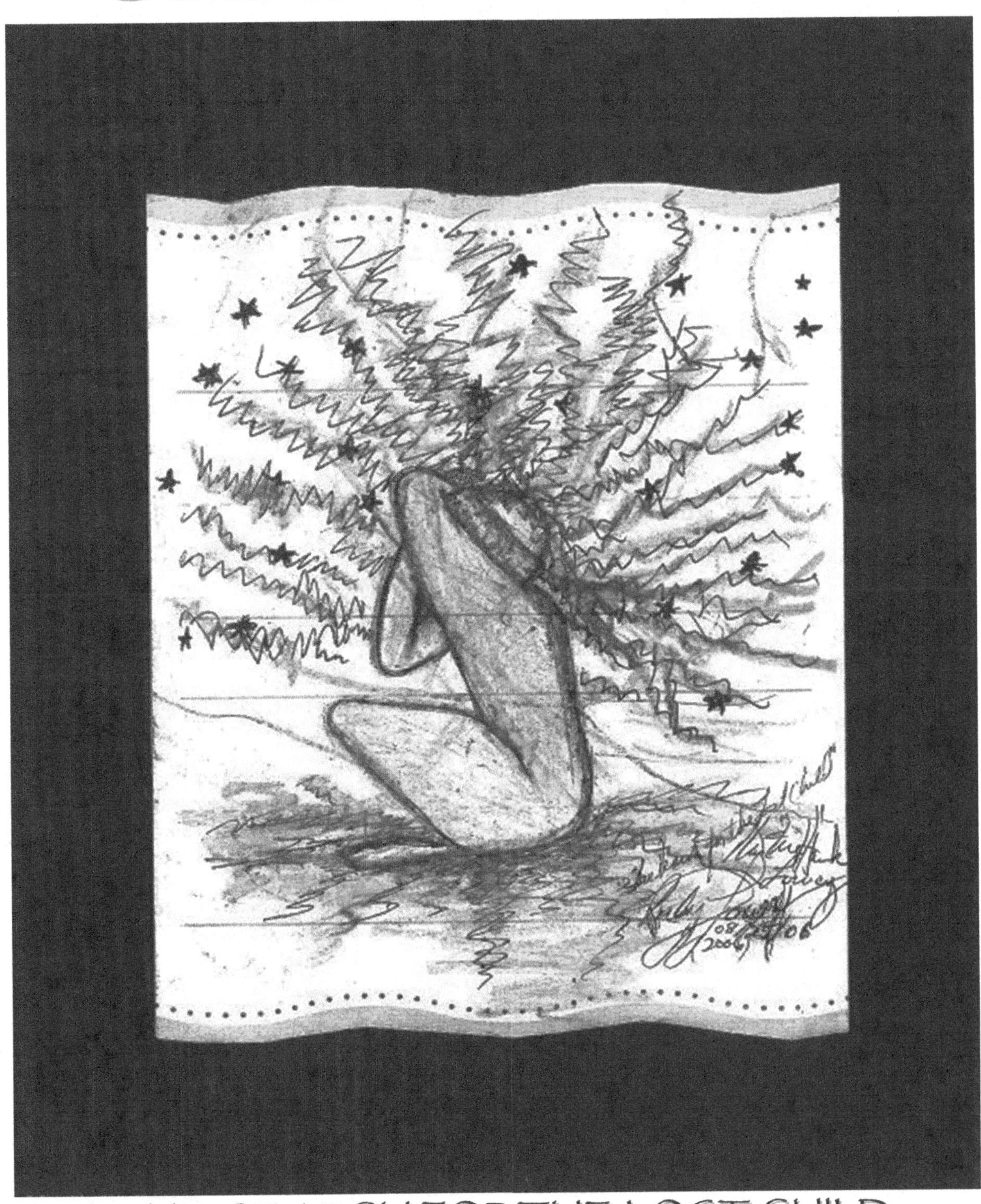

"THE SEARCH FOR THE LOST CHILD"

You are not lost.
You've merely
forgotten...

----The Author, Dr. R. Lowery-Hawk
February 21, 2011

...And the child looked up,

Saw the great sun
And the bright blue sky,
* *

And, she asked:
"Why does it shine so bright?"
"Feel so hot..?"

...And, the mother answered:
"Because it is LIFE, *and life you are..."*

Then night came upon them, and the child looked up,
Saw the full moon's glow, and the star's twinkling light,

And, she asked:
"Why does it glow so soft?"
"Feel so cool...? "

...And, the mother answered:
'Because... *it is* LIFE, and,

"LIFE, *YOU ARE!"*

"Questing"
Written: 1995

In the beginning,

Before time began, there was a great darkness,
And, that darkness was without form...

There was nothing but darkness, and so, there was nothing for darkness to reflex upon, nothing to touch, so as to relate to. Darkness was still unmoving; formless; and silent. Darkness was without substance, and, without dimension. Darkness was void...

This Great Darkness grew darker as it inhaled more of *It*-self, as more of *It*-self expanded... And so it was, that before long, darkness had touched darkness! Bumped right into *It*-self!

Darkness had done all this because *It* had gotten use to darkness, and so had to become darker in order to stay Dark. This act of going into *It*-self caused a change, and that change created: Motion! Motion caused Dark to touch dark; and so now there was Some-*thing* to relate to, and, to help Darkness **know** darkness. Darkness now greeted and took a look at *It*-self. Darkness finally found *It*-self and so, created a "Child". That child was a Child-Of-Motion that "gave birth" to The- Child-Of-Light...

That "Child of Light" was:

"SOLO"

"The Child of Motion"
Written: September 1995

IN THE STILLNESS, THERE LIES "SOLO"...

✡ ✡

Solo was very still and very lonely.

Solo never use to be lonely...

Where did lonely come from..?

Lonely came *AFTER* Solo "awoke."

While **Solo** "slept", **Solo** did not know lonely was around,

Nor, did **Solo** know that Solo "slept."

When Solo "stretched", "yawned and opened" The "eye", Solo saw "sparks" fly forth from Some-where. This Some-where was: Solo! (This was static electricity from Solo's "Eye's" movement in the dark.) The sparks gave Solo "Sight", and so,

Solo, saw that

Solo was...*ALL ALONE...*

Solo also seen that Solo **was** oval shaped in the form of what we'd call an...

EGG/EYE!

AS THE LONLINESS GREW, SOLO "GREW"

TO WANT TO FIND OTHERS LIKE SOLO.

Solo *felt* a great "bubble" fill up inside of Solo. This bubble was created from loneliness. The bubble wanted to get out! The Bubble grew and grew until it burst forth out of Solo! It came out with a mighty force that caused Solo to open Solo's eye wide! When Solo did this, Solo was conscience! Solo now looked with awareness straightforward. In doing this, Solo became aware of another space, (direction) of Solo's existence. This awareness moved from Solo out in a straight-line, sending conscience-ness into it. Amazed, Solo then felt a tug in back, to turn around in that direction (the one behind Solo.) Solo did! Solo was now brought aware of another space, (direction) and so, sent out conscience-ness there too. Now Solo was being strongly compelled to turn to the left and sent conscience-ness in that direction as well! After sending Solo's conscience-ness to the direction on Solo's left, Solo again felt a strong pulling desire to move. This "time", Solo was spun to the right, moving Solo pass the direction that had, in the beginning, been the direction in back of Solo! Solo, in this forth direction, again sends out conscience-ness. Next, Solo looks up, sending conscience-ness straight out and up! Solo was beginning to feel a pattern to things; a naturally instinctive nature of a sort, that now naturally lead Solo to look curiously beneath Solo. When Solo did,

Solo discover: Yes! Another direction was there! Solo then sent, straight down, a beam of conscience-ness. There now was created: six directions of conscience-ness in the dark void. This sixth direction completed an arrangement of "Some-things", (which did not exist until now) around Solo. Solo viewed it all, and felt it all. It felt cozy and comfortable...secure! (Solo now knew emotions/feelings.) Solo felt a feeling about it all. That feeling felt... *GOOD!* Solo looked upon Solo's creation and saw it was indeed good! The feeling was good! And, what Solo seen looked good, so then, Solo proclaimed it! Solo proclaimed: **ALL IS GOOD!** Solo was very pleased with these creations, and this pleasure produced in Solo: a large smile! With all this, Solo felt contentment and so, inhaled a large sign, inhaling along with it: Life! Solo then naturally released an exhale, and thus, breathed life back out to all directions! Solo was now looking in the sixth directions surrounding Solo. All this beautiful awareness provided the feelings of comfort and companionship to the once lonely Solo... The six directions of conscience surrounded Solo. Solo now rested in this surrounding bliss of conscience-ness created by the *ALL seeing eye* of Solo... Then...Solo paused for reflection. After an *unrealized* "time" had been spent pausing and enjoying the resting in the bliss, Solo began to feel a natural desire, like a need, to move again to discover what was at the end of the lines of conscience-ness that solo had projected into six directions. Curiosity and discovery was then birthed with Solo; and so, Solo moved again, curious, so beginning the first journey along the paths of each of the six directions!

Solo decided to begin Solo's first movement of exploring, in the first four directions of conscience-ness that Solo had sent out; then, move to the above and below direction. Solo then moved to the end of conscience-ness in each of the six directions, creating a line from one end's tip to the end tips of the other five; connecting them all together as six. Solo had moved to the end of each path. Next Solo connected each of the end points. With the moving to one end of a path, (direction) and then touching each of the six direction's ends to the next one, (after having previously traveling upon each one) Solo succeeded in connecting them all together as one. Solo had, by doing this, created geometric shapes of: a square, a diamond, a pyramid, and a triangle; that then became: an octahedron! Solo was now surrounded inside these geometric shapes Solo had created with Solo's movements. These projections of conscience-ness into the void had created the first Octahedron! Solo now sat within Solo's first creation. Solo had sat blissfully and still for quite a while, enjoying and experiencing, again the good of new and perfect *creation...* Then! Solo stirred again from Solo's restful bliss, and decided to *"awake"* and move, again! Solo was so happy with all this creation that a great joy welled up inside Solo! This joy was so great that it sent Solo to turning all around! This action gave way to Solo's wondering if the octahedron creation could spin also. Solo thought about this and instantly the octahedron began to spin with Solo remaining in a position of stillness inside. When the octahedron spun, it spun on three axes: front to back, left to right and up and down. When it spun around each of the three axes, the parameters became: a sphere! Solo was delighted! "I wonder if I can create another one just like this one? I'll create it just like the last one; same size; same shape; and then I'll spin it like I did this on, and create another sphere! The sphere looks a lot like me! It is in my likeness and I imagine (image) it so! It is then also in the image of me: how I (eye) *believe* I resemble my creation. Also, having the sphere around, I don't feel so lonely..." This was what Solo was thinking and feeling. Solo also wanted to see if Solo could again create all that had been created so far, and then, create more! Solo wanted to create more spheres so to keep Solo company. Solo had noticed that when octahedrons were created and spun on three axes, a sphere was formed. Solo also soon learned that Solo could move the octahedron with Solo inside or Solo could move Solo out of the octahedron and move around outside it. With that knowledge, Solo decided to go outside of the octahedron and create another duplicate of the previous one. Solo then moved to the top of the surface of the octahedron Solo was in. Solo then did the same things as before to create this new one that could spin and create a sphere that had the image in the likeness of Solo. It was successful! Now there were two octahedrons, the same *size and shape* as the first one! Solo is so joyful that Solo projects Solo's joy to the new octahedron, which sets it to spinning! Solo spins it through the *three axes* and creates another sphere! Solo then wanted the two sphere *"children" to come together* and see one another, so Solo moves the first sphere over to *intersect with the second sphere*. A special something happened then! When the two spheres intersected, a vesica piscis was formed! (The two spheres intersecting resembles two bubbles: a vesica piscis), *emerging as one.* As this happened something amazing occurred! A bright *"something"* came forth from it! This, Solo called: Light! What happened next was equally amazing! *The light brought forth, with it:* knowledge! Which Solo quickly absorbed!

Solo was enjoying Solo's existence and creations; and so, went on creating duplicates of what Solo had so far created. Solo was now observing all of Solo's creations, and this was teaching Solo much! Solo was gaining knowledge and was noticing, even more, the changes that were occurring since Solo first became aware of Solo. Solo was learning the ways of life! Solo moved forward, now, concentrating on discovering if Solo could move outside of the surrounding Solo creation. Soon, Solo found self outside of the octahedron-sphere that Solo had first created... And, it happened! Light *again* flew out from Solo and into the dark! Solo had noticed, after the light had come, that now, whenever Solo moved, more light was created! Solo remembered this, and all things Solo had experienced so far; so then, Solo chose to concentrate on the *memories* of making another movement in the dark void.

Solo concentrated and then experienced self moving *again* in the void! As Solo moved in the void, Light also moved. The Light moved *with* Solo!

* *

MADE SOLO HAPPY AND JOYFUL!
AND THAT CAUSED SOLO TO LAUGH!

An amazing thing happened when Solo laughed. When Solo laughed, Solo shook and shook! The more Solo shook, the more Light-Sparks flew! The more Light Sparks flew, the more Solo laughed! Solo then had to catch Solo's breath; and so then, inhaled to laugh some more! When this happened, another very amazing thing happened! Solo's Breath, that exhaled out from the laughter, caused Solo and the Sphere, Solo had put around Solo, to move forward! UP SHOT SOLO! Solo laughed more, and so inhaled.

DOWN SOLO WENT!

Then out he breathed, and up again he went! This continued on and on... And so, as Solo leaped up and down, sparks flew more brightly...The sparks began to move with Solo, following Solo because they liked the laughter and because, if they did not move with Solo, they would not be seen; and if they were not seen, they would be all alone...If they were all alone, they too, would be lonely. Solo went through the darkness laughing, moving up and down making Light. These Lights then also began to wiggle and to move. Because of this, their wiggle was sent back to Solo. Solo felt this movement that had come from *somewhere*. Solo then stopped laughing and began to *wonder*...Solo wondered about the movement it had felt. Solo wondered and Solo *thought* and thought...then... There it was again! Just at that moment, something pulled hard on Solo! Hard and quick! Solo was then thrown back the way Solo had just come! There had now come in Solo's world, *a point of change*...The change came in the shape of: a Spiral! *The Spiral Solo called: "Serpent Child;" "Serpent-Child" that emerged from Solo!* What was happening was: when the Lights wiggled, the Lights began to move also. Their movements grew stronger with each movement, soon becoming a great and powerful tug! When this tug happened, something powerful also happened: *Solo, was torn in two!* Solo was then "*opened up*" and, out of Solo came:

"A GREAT SERPENT"

'SERPENT BEGAN TO FALL DOWNWARD AND INTO THE DARKNESS...

Solo watched, in wonder, in confusion, worry, and then...sorrow, Solo's other half with the Lights following/attached to it, (as were they to the other half of Solo) drifting away, retracing the trail Solo had first paved. Solo floated motionless, still and shocked, watching the insides of Solo, (*Solo's* "Inner-self, *Solo's child")*, tumbling and tumbling downward, spinning in circles and spirals. Solo's "Inner-Self": "The Serpent", "The Child", spiraled continually downward; lost in darkness; moving further and further away from the "Oval Egg" known as: Solo...Solo had begun to move forward, to go after "Serpent". But "Serpent" had seemed to disappear, so fast did "Serpent" move! *Something* "wet" began to fall from Solo's "eye". This wetness from Solo's "eye" was: "tears". The "tears" now also began to "fall downwards" from Solo. As Solo's "tears" fell, the Light Spirals, that were with Solo's "detached other self half", were retracing backwards the patterned trail that Solo had first made in its laughter's movements. It was at one of these repeated movements that one of Solo's "tears" fell onto the "Light Trail". "The other half of Solo" and its "Spiraling Light Trail", at that moment, were directly beneath Solo, and so they were in line with Solo's "tears". Down fell Solo's "tears", and onto the "Electrical Light Spiral"! When this happened ***Some-Thing*** rose up to meet Solo. It felt *warm,* yet wet, and then it felt cool. This jotted Solo into wonderment *again!* "What was THAT!" Solo asked *self,* and immediately began *wondering upon it.* Solo's "wet tears" created "Mist"! It was after this, that Solo began to realize it was *again not* alone. Solo had soon come to the realization that there were things ***now*** around Solo that had not been there before. This made Solo very, very happy! Solo now did not feel as lonely as before. Solo began to think and think; and because of all this thinking, Solo now began to feel a desire stirring up inside Solo: Solo now wanted to go and find Solo's "inner-child self"! Solo remembered how to move, and Solo remembered how laughter had propelled it forward and then upwards... and so, Solo filled up Self with joy and laughter, and then laughed and laughed and laughed, breathing in then out! Solo then began to spiral *in search of "The-Inner-Child-Self"*: "The Serpent"! Solo had soon learned that if Solo thought about where Solo wanted to go, Solo could direct "Solo's Self" in that direction.

SOLO WAS LEARNING MANY THINGS...

Soon, another amazing thing began to happen: Solo's "Spiraling-Light-Trail" began to pause and then quiver and quiver. Next, waves began to move up the Spiral's Trail and towards Solo. The Trail began to throw out its own "Electrical Light" and... it "bumped" right into Solo! It "latched onto" Solo, and so, "followed" Solo in Solo's "search within the dark" to find "The Lost child". Now Solo had "two trails of Light" coming from Solo! The Light from Solo, ***plus*** the Light from Solo's "returned other half", now "lit" the way for Solo to "see". The Light was now "all around Solo". It lit the way before and behind Solo to where Solo once was, to where Solo was now heading to...

Solo searched and searched for a long, long "time", making Light Trails, (Paths) all through the darkness. As Solo did so, Solo could see more and more and better and better... These movements with more Light created "Sound", and so now Solo had even "more company". "The Sound"- did something to Solo. It caused Solo to tingle and vibrate all over! This caused Solo to move faster and faster! It made Solo feel more excited, more gleeful, and, hopeful!

NOW ALL THAT CAME TO BE FOLLOWEDOLO
IN THE SEARCH FOR: SOLO'S "LOST CHILD"...

✡ ✡

Eventually, Solo saw its "Lost Serpent-Inner-Child". Solo then called out to *The Light, to "The Sound", and to "The Steam of Mist"*, that had been created from Solo's "wet tears". Solo called out to all of these to help Solo to catch up to the "Lost Child". "Sound" hurried fast to Solo's beckoning call! When "Sound" did this a great *"Some-Thing"* hit from behind. This Some-Thing caused Solo to let out a great **"OOOFF!"** ***That*** became: **'Wind'**...

"Mighty Sound" had bumped right into "Misty Steam"! Then "Misty Steam" had bumped into "Electrical Lights"; and all these had bumped hard into Solo, creating "Wind"! "The Wind" caused Solo to roll. Solo felt Self roll over and over again, and right into "Serpent"! All this had happened because of the *"bump"*!

Solo quickly grabbed the "Serpent's tail"! This startled the "Unrepentant Serpent" who was "falling", lost, lonely, and frightened. This action jolted "Serpent" so greatly that the "Serpent's Mouth" flew open, and out of its "mouth" flew a "Ball" in the shape of another "Egg"! This then caused the "Serpent" to forget about Self and focus on "Ball". "What is that!" asked Serpent to Self. Serpent looked in wonder and curiosity at the "Egg-Ball" which had come forth from Serpent. The Egg Shaped "Ball" "glowed" brightly. Looking at this "Glowing Ball", "Serpent" thought: "If I go and get 'My Ball', I can ask what 'Ball' ***is***." Solo was observing "Serpent-Child" watching the "Egg-Ball" that had come forth from the "Serpent's Mouth"; because of this, Solo decided to try and break free from the "Serpent", so that "Serpent" could chase "Serpent's Ball" ("Egg") and discover what "Ball" ***is.***

THIS "EGG-BALL" WAS LIKE THE FIRST SHAPE
SOLO HAD SEEN SHAPED LIKE SOLO...

Solo had hurried so fast to catch "Serpent" that Solo bumped right into "Serpent"! "Serpent" did not even turn to see what it was that had bumped into "Serpent". "Serpent" therefore, did not *greet* Solo. "Serpent" did not acknowledge that Solo was even there! "Serpent" did not say to Solo: "Hello Solo, my 'Egg-Self'; my Creator: Mother/Father! I am so glad you are here! I missed you! I am wanting to stay with you and join your 'Dance with The Light in the dark'; helping you create all these unexpected wonders!" No, "Serpent" did not greet Solo. "Serpent" was *too curious*! And yet, Solo knew that "Serpent", like Solo, also felt sad for thinking that a part of "Serpent's Self" had left it, believing that part was its own "Inner-Child"...

THAT "INNER-CHILD" OF "SERPENT" WAS THE ""BALL OF LIGHT"

"Serpent", therefore, felt *strongly* that "Serpent" had to "catch Serpent's ball" and get to know all about "Ball"; learn what "Ball" was, and *why* "Ball" glowed. "Serpent" then began to *wonder again.* "Serpent" wondered: "If 'Ball' came out of 'Serpent', and 'Serpent' came out of 'Ball-Egg' called: Solo, what will come out of '*My* Ball'? What would then come out of what came out of "My Ball'? Oh, so much! So much to know and to experience and understand!" So, "Serpent" tugged and wiggled, and wiggled and tugged, trying to get away from Solo to find "Serpent's *missing part"*: the "Ball".

Solo said to "Serpent": "But 'Serpent', if you follow 'Ball' I'll have to *follow you;* and if I follow you, 'Wind' will have to follow me; and if 'Wind' follows me, 'Sound' will follow 'Wind'. 'Misty Steam' will then have to follow 'Sound', 'Tears' will follow 'Misty Steam', and 'Electric Light' will then have to follow 'My Tears'. 'My Tears' will next have to find and follow 'Me'. 'My Tears' will follow me, creating a *circle,* and I, Solo will again create more 'Tears', more 'Misty Steam', more 'Electric Light', and more 'Sound', and more 'Wind'. 'Wind' will be stronger and follow 'Ball'; that will make 'Ball' go further away from *you.* You will go after 'Ball', and where 'Ball' goes is 'Darkness'. We shall then be brought back again to 'Darkness'... 'Darkness' will then follow ALL of us! The faster we have to follow you, the more *we become...*yet, the more we become, 'the faster we move'; and, the faster we move, the more we *might tumble* over and over, 'loosing one another'; so then, the faster will 'Darkness': 'The Great Void', 'follow from behind'. If we move too fast in desperation to catch one another, the faster 'Darkness' shall 'catch up' with *us;* 'hitting us from behind'... If 'Darkness' 'bumps us from behind', 'Darkness' will then 'swallow us *all* up'! So search my 'Child', if you must, for 'Ball', but do it with *consideration of ALL* of the movements, and us, this will create. For, as we can 'see', *each* of us are 'giving birth' to '*Some-Thing*' new, and it's 'causing' *us* to become curious, and to wonder and ***wander.*** Too much thoughtless wandering can create a feeling of lost and separation. This creates 'lonely' with a great and *driving 'wanting'* to have what we had first created, back, again. What I have observed is: each time we act and re-act towards our newly created 'Child', we seem to then create a different kind of life form called: 'Our ***Lost*** Inner Child'. So we *must* try to think of *all of us,* not just our own personal curiosity, desires, and needs. Instead, we must try to find the *right* movements that will enable us to create a purposeful and smooth harmonious flow that is flavorful for *All.* One that does not jerk and knock us forcefully into one another, the way it has been happening so far. The forceful jerking causes us to push another '*Some-'Thing* forth that we, as a family, have not decided is a good and needed thing for *ALL of us* as a *whole unit* of movement and creation. Our decisions should be one that adds harmony and feelings of *completeness* to our 'Dance of Becoming' in the Void..." BUT, "SERPENT DID NOT PAUSE *TO LISTEN TO ITS ELDER* AND "PARENT": THE NOW MUCH WISER SOLO...

Solo had become knowledgeable, and wise, because Solo had experienced so many changes since it had first "awakened", and, because Solo had "taken The Time" to *ponder* them and learn from them. Solo had observed all that it "saw", and all that it "fel"t, and then gave it *all* some thought. Solo explored and questioned what Solo was "seeing" and experiencing. Solo then gained great insights and great wisdom; and from all of this, he became...

ALL KNOWING...

"Serpent" however, had not as yet, arrived at wisdom and knowing; and so, "Serpent", rather then moving *closer* to Solo, had moved further away; too far away to "hear" what Solo had been saying to "Serpent". "Serpent" moved on and "away" from Solo, seeking out its own "Egg-Shaped-Ball"; moving ever farther away from Solo... and farther form the "Light"...

"SERPENT WAS NOW IN DARKNESS, AND...SERPENT WAS ALL ALONE...

When "Serpent" finally came to realize this, "Serpent" became frightened and then began to finally feel how lonely, lonely can be when one's family of Light is absent and only "Darkness" in its place.

AND SO IT WAS, THAT "FEAR" THEN "MOVED WITHIN THE DARKNESS...

"Serpent" saw "The Glowing Ball", a tiny dot now, and this then became the only thing "Serpent" could "see". "Serpent" felt it now *HAD TO* follow "The Ball", for "The Ball" reminded "Serpent" of "Home"... of Solo. Home was Solo! "Serpent" now missed Solo. "Serpent" was finally beginning to come to the realization that Solo had felt about "Serpent" (Solo's "Inner-Serpent-Child") the same way "Serpent" was feeling about "Serpent's" "Inner-Ball-Child". "Serpent" **now** paused, for "Serpent" was beginning to realize that Solo had wanted "Serpent", in the same way, and with the same passion, that "Serpent" wanted his own "Child-Self": "The "Ball". "Oh", "Serpent" thought, "If only I had of 'listened'! I could have had Family, Love, and Light! I could have had company instead of loneliness. Solo might have also helped me find 'Ball'. If we had found 'Ball' we might have been able to of learned of 'The Ball-Child'. If a 'Child' should come from 'Ball-Child', we then might have come to understand the 'child' and us, and what all this means. Together, then, we might have been able to have watched and learned of and about all the other new births' Becoming".

AND SO, *THE "LOST SERPENT-CHILD" IS ALWAYS TRYING TO "CATCH " ITS BALL-CHILD"...*

After a time, "Serpent" said to "Self": "Maybe 'Ball' will be wiser than me; and since 'Ball' glows like Light, Maybe 'Ball' will find Light and then lead me back home to Solo..." And so it is, that "Serpent" now must follow "Ball", always afraid of the dark, afraid of being all alone and left behind and unable to find the way back "home" to "Serpent's" first original Self: Solo; and back to the other new creations. Mean while, each time Solo tries to find the lost "Inner-Child", Solo gets "bumped from behind and tumbles". This causes "A Great Jerk" on Solo, and so, "a part of Solo is ripped in half"; and then "out comes another "Serpent-Child-Self" creation! "Falling away" in a spiraling formation, lost in the darkness, with Solo and Solo's other selves in pursuit"; concerned for the "*Falling Children*", "searching for them, to bring them, back home..." But Solo and the other "Evolving" "Serpents" (Spirals) and "Balls" ("Eggs"/Spheres), are also being "re-attached" each time they move with Life, and with that, a "new Light

trail" (path) is created to help Solo find "Serpent", and to help "Serpent" find "Ball". "The Light Trails" are to guide all newly created "Children" that "spring forth" to: *SOLO...*

Solo remembers the first movement and how dark, Dark is. Solo also remembers First Child: "Serpent-Spiral"; and when Solo does, Solo begins to "cry"...and when Solo "cries", Solo creates "wet tears" that "*fall and fall, hitting*" "Electrical Light", and "*pulling* Magnetic Light energy", bringing new Life forth and into action; creating more and more: **Life!** This new Life is all that ***is***, and all that ***is*** then begins to move faster and faster! So, then...Solo ***must*** try and remind, teach and train ALL of the new forms of Life on how to move smoothly in rhythm and in harmony. If Solo does not reach enough of Solo's "Children and their creations", all then will collide into one another, "devouring one another"; and if this impact, "This Great Bump", is hard enough...then what? Could Solo be *swallowed up by the Dark Void?*

WHAT THEN?

"Oh", Solo said. "Oh! Oh! I hurt and feel sick inside! I miss and worry so for My Children!" Solo then "cried", making more "Tears", more "Misty Steam", and more "Sound and Light", to join with "The Electrical Light" Solo created as Solo moved through the dark and "Void". All these Elements reacted, and so, more Life Forms were propelled into Motion. More creation created, therefore, more for Solo to attempt to reach and train. Solo would do this by aid of" **Electrical Light**".

Solo had to learn, by way of ***Memories***, to be happy again, to laugh again, and to create enough "Electrical Light" so as to be able to "see" to try and keep **"Darkness" equal to "Light"...**

YET, WHEN SOLO CREATED MORE LIGHT, IT DREW DARK NEARER...

And, so it was, that Solo knew that the only hope for *ALL* that had been created so far, and ALL that would continue to be created, was for Solo to stay calm and give ***all*** some thought, then try and communicate with the other Creations. By doing so, and by staying aware of Solo's Creations and what was also happening "inside of them", including Solo, Solo would be able to communicate, by way of thought, with Solo's Creations. Solo had come to the reasoning that, by doing this, a "Life-Line" would be created, connecting Solo to all of Solo's Creations. This "umbilical-life-line" would remain "open" as long as the others *sought* Solo and *desired to return, to create together*, in harmony and order of balance. This would be possible because *ALL creation came from Solo*. "Perhaps", Solo reasoned to Self, "If I do this, and keep the movements of My-Self, (which is this Some-*Thing* I now call: Life-Force-Energy), moving smoothly in rhythm and Love with *no fear*, I'll then always have that "open line" for *ALL My Children to sense* and to *remember* in order that they might find a way to move also in this smooth and serene, rhythmic, flowing motion; creating harmonious Life as they and I do so.

For, perhaps that is what I should now do rather then worrying about whether they shall return back to me...back to: **"Home".**

Because of Solo's search, Solo had extended Conscience-ness. Conscience-ness went where Solo went, therefore, Solo's looking and seeking extended conscience in all directions. The more conscience-ness was extended, the more Solo became aware of things to ponder upon. From pondering, Solo got ideas; and ideas helped make more "Things" to create. One of the ideas Solo got was for Solo to go back inside the octahedron, *"bathe" in its energy and allow it to calm and sooth Solo's concerns*. When Solo achieves that, Solo decided, Solo should then *spin it*.

Solo went back to the octahedron, moved inside, and became tranquil... As Solo "bathed" in this feeling, something amazing happen! Solo, began to: "dream"...the Pondering-Dream gave Solo visions, and possibilities! Solo's ponderings moved to imaging (Imagination/creativity), and Solo then began to create "*The Dream*"! Solo now knew how to reach "The Lost Children"! Solo now, could show them the way back to Solo! Solo would give them choice (free will): the freedom to make choices. It would be the rights and privilege of each Creation's readiness to make their *own* choice when to return back to their Source and Creator: Solo! Solo understood *now* that the "Children" too, being like Solo, and a part of Solo, would also desired to do all the things Solo desired to do. So, since Solo now knew Love, Solo expressed it to *all* of Solo's Creations; and one of these ways of expression was to *allow* each Creation to arrive at its *own "time" of choice*. Solo had wanted to find the "Lost Serpent" and any other "Children" "springing" forth from "Serpent". But, Solo now realized it would be very challenging, complicated, and frustrating for Solo to do this, when more Life was forever being created because of Solo's search; for they were also creating more new Life Forms, all which had to also be taught: The Dance of Rhythm and Harmony. It was far better, Solo decided, if Solo simply allowed them to find their own way back, when they, themselves felt the urge to do so; applying their own free will (choice). Solo decided it would be good for Solo to learn patience, trust and faith, which would enable Solo to wait for their return. And, at that moment of their return, Solo would most happily and Lovingly welcome them back! For Solo had learned, along the way of Solo's becoming, trust, faith and compassion; and along with that, Solo had experienced and felt, and therefore, created: ***Love***...

SOLO WAS BECOMING EVER MOMENT,
EVER WISER, EVER MORE: LOVE!

Solo understood ***now*** that "Solo's Children" would "journey out" again and again after they had "found" Solo; for this would now be a natural motion-thing of co-creating. "Solo's Children" were "duplicates of Solo", and as such, these Creations: "Solo's Children", were therefore, also "Creators" of new Life. Solo now understood that in order for the Solo's Creations to "survive", Solo needed to communicate to them "*The Memories*", (Solo's Memories). Those memories were not about *their* beginnings alone, but also about *ALL* Creation's *Beginnings*. "The Memories" were also about each Creation's Purpose in Life. Solo had learned to send thoughts into the "Dream", and therefore, decided to try and send out a Message (telepathically, in "The Dream") to "The Serpent" ("Spiral") and to ALL "Serpents", ALL "Balls", (Life-Light), and ALL of Solo's "Off Springs" (Creations) in *every form*. The Message was: for them to seek Solo, "The First Cause", "The First Realized and Crystallized Form, and Awareness of Self From the Deep Void". Solo decided to also send a Message, telling them: they are all apart of *The One*; and that one is: Solo; they need to learn the movements and the flow that unites them ALL in: thought, harmonic Love, Light, Creation, and Companionship. That unites them, each and every one to:

The All of Every-Thing, and to ***The No-Thing of All...***

This was the way of things...

This was:

"*THE DANCE OF LIFE!*"

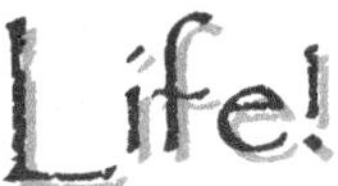

* Solo must not get "swallowed up"! For the sake of *ALL of them!* AND, For the sake of *Existence*...called:

Life!

✡ ✡

Solo must stay in Existence, even if ALL others are "swallowed up". It would create great sorrow and grief for Solo to loose ALL Life-Family *so far created;* but, if Solo too is "devoured", then there would be "No-Light" to "*see*" to: "Come Home" to.

And,

There would be "No-Home" to come back to. There would then *again,* be "only" "Dark-ness" and "The No-thing-ness" of:

The Great "Void"

Written: September 1995

*Many of the words in the story of SOLO, were * written in bold. These were the "things" becoming.

* **SOLO**: "Cosmic Egg"; "Creator's All Seeing Eye"; "First Light"; "First Cause" *
* **SERPENT**: Spirit; Spiraling Light; life/creation; Kundalini; Universe; Galaxy *

(See Glossary for more definitions.)

* ***THEY MEAN MUCH MORE; BUT THAT'S FOR YOU TO RECALL, AND SO, KNOW…***

"I praise you Father of Heaven, Lord of Earth; that you've hidden these things from the wise and the intelligent, and have revealed them to babes."

----From the Christian bible

Then night came upon them, its darkness descending, making, veiling, for a time,

Their memories...

Lost in their "Shadows" of the illusions of separation, they lost sight of their origin, lost sight of their innocence, and so, lost sight of them... (Spirit) They then "painted masks" and covered their faces with their illusions, awaiting the time when their 'innocence' would once more awaken and...

remember...

One by one, each of their multiples of "masks" would be removed in the search for the truths of life's origins, and so then, the truths, of them... Through their "Shadows of Death" and their "Lights of Birth" do they journey, to "fall and to rise", blindly stumbling and hiding; seeking and grasping understanding; until willfully removing their "masks" of illusions and fears.

One by one, singing and dancing the masked veils away, reviving their

Divine "Child" within

Reviving their "child of innocence" and wonder,
Understanding IS then gifted...

Understanding then gained, illusion dropped,
The "Child" awoke, and then...

"THE CHILD LOOKED UP"...

"The Awakening"
Written: 1995

"*ALL* ARE CHILDREN IN THE EYES OF GOD"

—The Author,
July 04, 2011

LOOK AT LIFE IN THE SILENCE,
THROUGH THE EYES OF WONDER
AND IMAGINATION...

IMAGINE MORE....

—The Author
July 08, 2012
Sunday, 12: 13 A.M.

"Look well into yourself;
There is a source,
Which will always spring up,
If you will search there."

--------*Marcus Antonius*

READER'S OWN IN-SPIRED WRITINGS

****

READER'S OWN IN-SPIRED WRITINGS

****

CHAPTER THREE

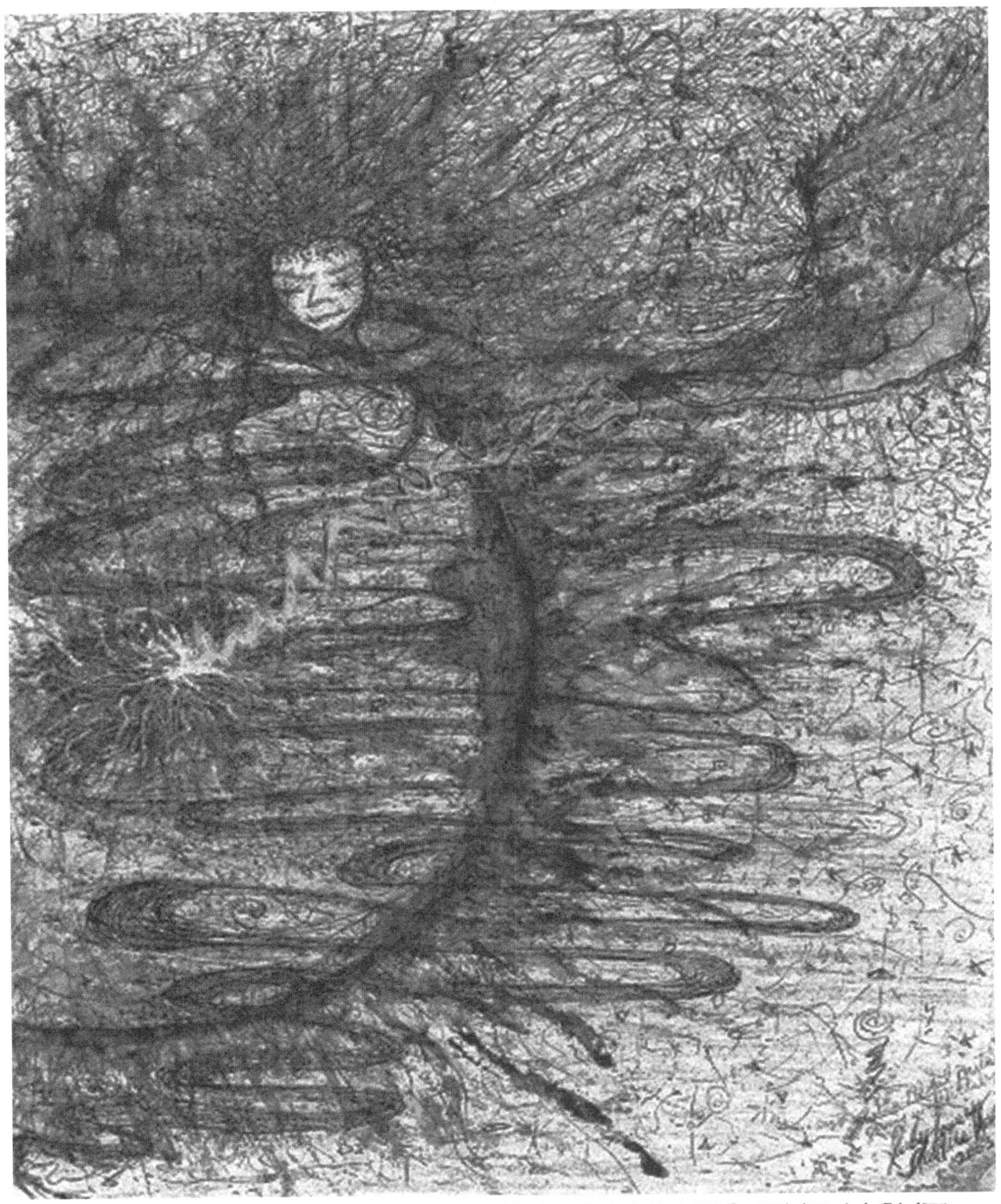

"AND THE MIST PARTED, GIVING WAY TO THE LIGHT"

The Great Spirit is in all things; he is in the air we breathe. The Great Spirit is our Father, but the Earth is our Mother. She nourishes us; that which we put into the ground she returns to us....

----Big Thunder (Bedagi)
(late 19th century)
Wabanaki Algonquin

SILENCE…

The Quiet unknown,

STILLNESS…

The Great Eternal Pause…

THEN…

Came the exhale,

THE SIGH,

Which became the Breath that moved

ACROSS

THE GREAT VOID…

Its sound became

The Word;

And The Word

became…

"THE MIST"…

"The Word, The Mist"
Written: 1991

...And the fog moved in,

covering all that it touched. Dampness followed, clinging to that which it met. In its quietness, its Unknown mystery, Ignorance was born, and so birthed: *FEAR...*

Then the Sun showed its "face", and calm began its breath across The Great Void... Bright Rays of Light caressed the Mist and Drew It up into the embrace of The Heavens...

AND SO, FOR A TIME, THE MYSTERY WAS FORGOTTEN...

But... the "Heart Beat" returned; The Breath moved; and The Cycle spun its Circle...

AND THEN...

THE HEAVENS WATCHED...

Heaven's "eyes" looked down upon the world of Matter.

The Fire Light from their "eyes" shone,

And the mystery deepened...

There, in the Heavens, the Gods delivered council,

Where as, one took his "staff" of power and cast it to the Earth!

The bolt of light streaked steadily across the Heavens to touch,

The "Heart of Earth"...

FIRE THEN DREW ITS FIRST BREATH ACROSS THE VOID, OF THE LONELY SKY...

The fire grew; the unknown grew; and so with it grew:

FEAR AND IGNORANCE!

Light "danced with fire", and so joined in:

"THE DANCE OF BECOMING!"

...THEN, THE GOD'S OOKED DOWN FROM THEIR HEAVENS, AND, THEIR EYES SHONE...

The Sun again returned and showed its "face" behind the clouds. The Sun spoke, The Night listened, and yielded to it's other 'Face"; yielded to its other "voice"... THE FIRE REMAINED, THE BREATH MOVED, THE MIST LINGERED; THE SUN WELCOMED THE POWER AS ITS OWN...

AWARENESS **then was born,** and moved across the land...
People "looked up"; they sang, and... their dancing began!
In anticipation, the night was welcomed back in its greetings to the LIGHT OF LIIFE; and, the MISTY FOG visited to **spread its touch, to Spread its "Mist - Mystery"**, to deliver its own GIFT OF LIFE...
The starry "eyes" of the "Gods" watched and were *PLEASED!*
ALL WAS GOOD !

The Heavenly Gods" looked down upon Creation, and their "DIVINE EYES OF FIRE LIGHT" BLESSED ALL THAT WAS SEEN,
And so, shared with them:

THEIR DIVINE SOULS...

All then were ONE!

AND THEN...

"The Gods Smiled"...

"The Gods smiled"
Written: 1997

The American Indian is of the soil, whether it be the region of forests, plains, pueblos, or mesas. He fits into the landscape, for the hand that fashioned the continents also fashioned the man for his surroundings. He once grew as naturally as the wild sunflowers; he belongs just as the buffalo belongs...

Luther Standing Bear, 1868? -1939) - Oglala Sioux Chief

The Light was bright, brilliant...

But it was not a light, as we know it now...

The Light was warm,

If there could have been the sensation

Of warmth then.

The Light was energy,

Yet, there was "no energy".

The Light was pure

And "contained nothing" but

Absolute Truth and Goodness.

THE LIGHT WAS HOLY...

The Light began, yet it never began.

The Light moved, and yet, it never moved.

The Light was "everything", And, yet,

It was "no-thing"...

The Light "split", yet, it never "split".

The Light was a "mind"...

Or, at least a mind, as we would think of it today.

It had a "force behind it, within it,

Around it".

It was "everywhere"...

And yet, it was *"no where"*.

It would take "time" and "no-where" to "emerge and fuse together",

before "nothing" could "join with everything".

Thus, "everything" would be "born", and "time" along with

"somewhere" would come into existence.

THE "LIGHT" WAS KNOWN AS: "LOVE"
THE "LOVE" WAS KNOWN AS: "I AM"

It was "I AM" who chose to "change",

It was "I AM" who chose to "multiply".

"I AM" became "everything",

"everything" "became:

"I AM".

"You are me, and I AM you. We are ONE,

And, yet, we are 'separate'.

We are ONE,

And yet, we are "MANY"!

"I AM" began to "evolve".

"I AM" became "Much", yet, "I AM" still "stayed": "I AM".

"Nothing" was taken away,

Yet, "Something" was given.

"I AM" was still as strong, yet, "The Many" were "*Weak*".

"The Many" "Weak", yet "Strong",

But, in comparison with the "ONE I AM",

The "many" were as "*crumbs from a cookie*":

The "same", but, yet, not "The Same".

"GOOD", but, not as good.

"POWERFUL," But yet... ***"not so powerful"...***

"I AM" "began" "The Change": "ONE Spark" was sent off in "ONE direction", "another in another direction", and "others" In yet, "other directions," other then *"THAT!"*

"Little Sparks" of "Light", from the "Big Spark of Light".

"The Light", "The Sparks" were "LIFE,
And yet, they were "NOT LIFE"!
Each "Spark" began to "change", to "rotate", to "spin", to "twist,"
to "swirl", until "MOTION" was "born";
And out of motion was born: *"LIFE"!*
The Life Force" was an "Energy Force".
"The Energy Force" was a "Thinking Force".
It "caressed" "Everything",

And yet, "Everything" was "not yet born". "Everything" had to be "born", but "Everything" could not be "born" until "Time" and "No Where" "came into" "existence", and "mated" as: *"ONE".* Thus, "Energy" had to "fuse" into "Time", and "No- Where" in order to have "Everything", which was "known" as: *"LIFE"* "come" "into existence". Since "Energy" "fused into" "Time" and "No Where", and "Time" and "No Where" had "Energy" and then "fused into" "Everything"", "Everything" then became also: *"ENERGY"*...

So we have it: "Everything" *"IS"* "LOVE";
"Everything" *"IS LIFE"!*
There "IS" "no" difference. "Everything" "blended together."
"Everything" was *"Still"* "I AM"... yet *"Changed"*

"I AM" was "Becoming Many Things..." "Many Things" began to "spring" from "Everything", because "Everything" began to "divide It Self" into "Something", and "Something" in turn divided "It Self" "first into": *"ELEMENTS"* The Elements took upon names.

Their names were: *FIRE; WIND; WATER; EARTH,* And *WOOD!*
These became *SPIRIT.*

Next, "Something' "divided into" *"Clans".* Those "Clan-doms" too, took upon names: *MINERAL, VEGETAABLE, ANIMAL, FUNGI, and BATERIAL,* and there multiplied into other *CIAN-DOMS".*

To aid these Clan-doms there would be *"DEVAS" ("Earth Spirits")* who were "Children" of "Everything" and "Something". These Devas were "small Beings" who consisted of a faster and higher vibrating Light then the other Clan-doms. These Devas, therefore, would become "*The Guardians of the Elements*" and other "Clan-doms"... ALL, except for a species of the "Animal" "Clan-dom"... In the "Animal Clan-dom" there became a "species" that was far "greater" in "reasoning and mobility" then any of the other "animals" in the animal Clans.

This species became known today as: *Man/Woman:*

Human Beings!

The "Guardians", Guides, and Angels" of the humans, dwelled in a "Clan-dom" "above" (Home of The Higher Light), and of a *"Higher Light"* frequency then the Physical Plane".

"I AM" "looked" at "Everything" and *"I AM"* "Saw" that "Everything" was: *"GOOD"...*

"Everything" was "Good", "Everything" was "Perfect";

"Everything" Was "in HARMONY"...

"I AM" had "become" "Much!" "I AM" had "become" *"EVERYTHING".*

"I AM" was ABUNDANCE!

"I AM" could now share with "I AM": "I AM's self":

"The *ONE*" "Bright Light": "I AM", would "rule" the "lesser Selves": the many "changing" "Sparks" of: "I AM".
With "Everything" in "Harmony",
"Everything" was therefore, *DININE!*
With "DIVINE" there was "No Wrong", Therefore,
"Wrong" was not "born".
Because "Wrong" had not yet "come into being",
"Everything" was therefore: *"PEACE"...*
"Everything was *"PURE";*
"Everything" was *"JOY", and "SPLENDER*
"EVERYTHING" WAS "PARADISE"!

"I AM" "smiled", thus, "SMILE" was "born". *"I AM" "SAW",* thus, "SIGHT" was "born". With "Sight" there came "BEAUTY" ; with "Beauty" there came "COLOR" therefore, "Color" was now "born". Every "Color" gave off "ENERGY", and this "Energy" gave off "VIBRATIONS!" These "Vibrations" could be "felt" and could "emerge into" the "Animal Clan-dom", blending with them to create *"Good Feelings"* in the "Animals": *"PURITY, CALMNESS, GOODNESS, PATIENCE, LOVE,* and *STABILITY",* along with *"Much More."* These could "help" *"create"* many *"Emotions",* therefore, "Emotions" were "born". Upon "seeing" all this "work", all this Creation, "I AM" "thought":

"ALL IS GOOD!"

"I AM" "thought": *"ALL IS good", therefore, I shall let* "ALL" *be "born".* "Go forth all my 'Children' *'and be' 'Abundance'.* Multiply 'within yourselves', and 'within your own species'. Keep in *'Divine*

Order' and 'ALL' that 'IS' 'needed' shall come to 'ALL'. Whatever your 'needs' whatever your 'desires', 'call' upon me 'FIRST', as I shall 'work' with you and 'through you'. As 'many' you will be 'strong', although 'weak', but as a 'whole' we become 'MIGHTY'! We MUST ALWAYS 'work' together. Keep this 'Harmony', this 'Balance'. Do not 'disturb' this 'Delicate Balance', this:

DIVINE ORDER'!

'Everything' is as it should be. Do not 'taste' of the 'fruits of Imbalance', do not 'disturb' 'order', do not allow 'wrong' to 'spring forth', for it will 'disturb' Your 'Faith'. All of 'Paradise' then shall 'suffer'. 'Paradise' will not be as you know it now. Do not 'disturb' your 'faith', for it IS your 'faith' that 'gives you' 'Paradise'. 'Disturb faith' and *'Confusion'* shall be 'born'. 'Confusion' IS the *'Brother of Wrong'*. They both are the *'Enemies of Good', 'Harmony', and 'Divine'*. If disturbed, *'battles'* will develop between them, and it *IS* these 'Battles' that shall *'destroy' 'Paradise'*! These 'battles' will linger for 'Eons of Time' before *'Everything'* can once more 'learn to *conquer' 'Wrong and Confusion'*; for 'Wrong' and *'Confusion' will multiply and become: 'Envy, Jealously, Anger, Hate, Doubt, and Worry'. 'Doubt' and 'Worry' will be the 'Parents' of 'Anger'; 'Hate'; 'Jealousy' and 'Envy'*. There will be *many 'Wrongs' and many 'Battles' for 'ALL'*. Therefore: *BE FAITHFUL; BE HAPPY;*

BE AT PEACE!'

Remember what I have told you: 'MY Children'.

Remember it well, for *this IS 'The Secret of 'Paradise'!*

This should be the 'state' of your 'mind'.

This *IS* your *'HEAVEN'!*

REJOICE'!

"REJOICE WITH EVERYTHING!

"I AM LOVE"
Written: Summer
1984, 4:00 A.M.

...And, the Light was Beauty;
And beauty was the light.

Song was the first sound,
And Beauty's first voice.
Its beginning radiated Light.
Life was Light and Beauty;
And all were:
ONE...

---THE AUTHOR
August 02, 2011

* *

In The Heavens,

There could be seen "Two Moons" but no "Stars"...
The "Moons" were: one "Full", the other: a "Sliver..."
'TWINS', same, yet different...
One printed with its time to *BE,*
The other: *READY TO DELIVER!*
BOTH "held" the Heavens together.
"All" was well, for ALL was **"just beginning..."**

As the Heavens "cradled" the "Two Moons", rocking them in its embrace of motion, the "Moons" also "began" to "rock". Each motion slowly shifted "The Twins" apart, until there came a moment that one "Twin Moon" was "across from the other"; there they saw the other's "face", and in "fear", they "covered" their own.

IT WAS THEN THEY REALIZED...
THEY WERE NOT ALONE...

Each moment one would prove to "peek out" and "see" its other "Twin-Self", the other would "hide". The "Full Moon" "thought" that the "Slivery New Moon" was about to "disappear", so small was Her Light. The "Slivery new Moon" "thought" the "Full Moon" would "consume" all of her, so large was Her Light...

SO THE PATTERN WAS FORMED: COURAGE AND CURIOSITY, FEAR, AND ILLUSSIONS.

This went on for a long, long while...

Until finally, "Time" had no place to go, so "time moved on..." As "time drifted" way pass "NOW", it "left" the "Two Moons" and "wandered" in "Darkness". "Time could not go back", nor could it "go forward", for there was "no Light" to 'See', therefore, "Stars" were then "put into" the "Darkened Heavens..." And so "began":

"The First Dance":

"THE DANCE OF BECOMING..."

Written: September, 1997

READER'S OWN IN-SPIRED WRITINGS

****

READER'S OWN IN-SPIRED WRITINGS

****

CHAPTER FOUR

"WEAVING THE MEMORIES, WEAVING THE DREAM..."
The Golden-Grand Mother-Spider-Woman)

✡ ✡

We are sometimes confused
By the way some things,
And some people "come" at us,
But it *is* in those
Moments, *Truth* calls to us...

The Author,
Tuesday, February 08, 2011
10:18 P.M.

(The Author communicating with the Great Mystery)

AUTHOR: "Why is it that when things seem to be going good, validating for me that I'm understanding life and you; things then seem to take a 'back swing', seeming then to confuse me and bring about doubts in what I was beginning to believe? Things then seem to be validating that all that you have shown me, and told me, is but non-sense, not true, but rather, only my imaginings.

Why? What is this?"

THE GREAT MYSTERY (GOD/GODDESS CREATOR): "Life is this. It is movement and rhythm. It is 'in and out', 'back and forth', 'round and about', 'up and down'... *ALL* lead to me. All move towards me, then back again to creating. To create one must 'dance' once more on the 'dance floor' of experience, and so KNOW. One cannot create that in which one does not know nor fully understand. One can create unknowns, but then if they do not come together well, they then must be 'changed' until they are 'perfected' into the movements and the 'breathe' of harmonious creation. When you grasp the essence of Truth, you come into realization. You then think upon it, and draw it into your reality. Once there, you try out your 'wings'. To help you learn the 'needed things', the 'fundamentals of necessity', I bring to you 'tests' of strength and Spirit. It is practice. Your newness then, to something just revealed or learned, may not be fully accepted by you as truth, even though you think you have done that. Because of that, you draw to you your doubts. You draw to you your old habits of doubts and fears. These then come to 'ask' of you: 'which is your truth?' You then must experience again where you were in the 'dark' before the 'Light of Truth' came to your 'memory'. Then you must decide whether to except either the pass beliefs as Truth, or the 'awaken' ones. You are 'up against' more then just *YOUR* own negative thinking and your own destructive belief patterns. You're 'up against' the masses of similar thinking cast forth into the 'dream': this place that you are experiencing that is created by all of your's and other's thinking and belief patterns; what they *'HOLD'* to be true. All of mankind is thinking, feeling and speaking things into creation, into being, creating more life forms; and each playing their part in it. Majority wins...or *THINKS* and believes they win; for the majority is the greater sum of the thinking and believing, and so, over-rides the minority's thinking and believing. When you have established your new way of thinking and believing, that is not necessary the same as most others awareness, you then will go for a time against the majority's group mind, and the unconscious grid that surrounds this planet, and so, for a time, you'll break free from them, and thus, see and feel the results of your thinking, and the results of your personal Truths. The majority of thoughts from the masses will return to you by way of the law of attraction---attaching to you, seeking out similar thought forms, to share life with. Habit Thinking, that has been with you, for a long time, becomes part of you. This law of attraction will therefore give those old thoughts power once more... *IF,* they find no 'resistance', by way of *NON-Acceptance.* You should not accept what you do not desire to keep. Do not accept it as your Truth nor your world. Until you ***allow*** yourself to realize the Truths of Love, the Truths of you, and the Truths of me, AND ***stick with them,*** you will keep on experiencing more of what Love is ***NOT*** rather then what ***Love IS***. You and all others are in the habit of 'falling asleep'. Do not give up, for it is in repetition one forms habits, and habits become your 'Guide'. Let your Guide be the good and the strength of Spirit, beauty, and purpose; moving you and life towards balance. Let your habits then form rhythm of a balanced Love-'Dance'. Allow each chaotic experience to 'awaken' you to that purpose! With each of your attempts to stay calm, trusting the Good and the Beauty, while focusing upon that plan, you will then eventually become more convinced of what I have been re-calling to you. It is by way of doing this that you shall 'ride' the waves of the 'back-ward slap' and 'ride' them as an exciting adventure of learning, creating and experiencing; towards your evolution of becoming all that you are meant to be...

All that I Am:
My Children in the likeness of me,
CREATING:

"IMAGES OF ME"...

Written: 2004

THERE CAME A BRIGHT LIGHT,
AND FROM OUT OF THE LIGHT,
THERE CAME A MIGHTY VOICE, PROCLAIMING:

"I'VE COME SO THOU MIGHT 'SEE',

Not That which thou
THINKETH,
But that which thou

"REMEMBERTH"...

---MESSAGE FROM THE GREAT MYSTERY
1990

CREATOR I AM...

For:
I AM THE "DREAMER":
The "Dreamer" that Dreams"---
I AM THE MAKER:
The Maker of Scenes---
I AM THE PRODUCER:
"The Movie"; "The Script; The Life"---
I AM THE CREATOR:
"Destroyer; The Light"--
YOU ARE THE "DREAMER":
"The Dreamer that dreams"---
ALL THAT YOU "SEE":
IS to YOU what it seems---
YOU make it; YOU shape it;
YOU create as you go---
YOU ARE "THE DREAMER":
YOU "Dream", YOU focus it so ---
YOU ARE "THE DREAMER":
"The Dreamer that Dreams"---
YOU ARE THE MAKER:
The maker of scenes ---
YOU ARE THE PRODUCER:
"The Movie, the Script, the Life"---
YOU ARE THE CREATOR:
"Destroyer, the Light"--

"THE DREAMER"
(From the Great Mystery)
Written: 1999

The Particles moved around and about,
They played to and fro—
They moved ever here and there,
They awaited a place to go---
A thought went out,
A Creator of a source---
And so, the Particles in play,
Hastened, along that creating course---
They quickly hastened to the thought,
Forming their Selves along the way---
Their purpose led them to their goal,
Creating forms, as they play---
The Sender's call had gone out,
So what else could they do?
The Particles were Life Stuff,
And Life they hastened to---
They gathered around that viberal thought,
Forming it as they do---
And so the "Hands" of form took shape,
The Particles becoming, that form too---
The Particles lived within the thought' domain,
Doing whatever it asked them to---
And so, played now, inside the new form,
Forming, according, to those thoughts, held true--

"PARTICLES"
Written: August 1999

"THE GREAT WONDERING AND IF-ING"

I wonder where Creation comes from?

What IF: all things start at a point of nothingness, and this nothingness IS REALLY *Some-thing...?*

What IF:

Our meaning and our understanding of the word no-thing-ness simply means: Some-thing ***beyond*** our hearing, seeing, touching, and smelling; something beyond the bodily senses that we have developed so far? And...

What IF:

For every nothing there is another nothing, but each Nothing is a Something? And, ***What IF:***

The nothings are *something* to other life forms?

What IF:

The word, another, stands for that?

What IF:

These other life forms' some things are more vast and more plentiful then ours? And, so, ***What IF:***

They then see less "*nothings*" then we do?

I wonder then what Nothingness is?

What IF:

Nothingness is like a tunnel that opens like a collapsing eye lens, and like a collapsing telescope adding new links to it faster then we are capable of comprehending for now? ***What IF:***

nothingness then creates such a movement that things begin to speed up? And, ***What IF:***

Speed is a funnel in the shape of a spiral: in the shape of an extended tunnel? So then... ***I wonder IF:***

Nothingness then is like a black hole of intense twirling movement that some might call: Wind, and some might call: Energy, while others might call it: energy swirling and sucking with a vacuum action. But,

What IF:

Wind and Energy, and the sucking vacuum action, are one and the same, only having different degrees of speed? And,

What IF:

It is *THIS* that creates?

What IF:

In truth there is no Nothing with nothing; only a nothing with such stillness that we, within our personal evolution of this so called "reality", have not yet "evolved" enough to sense its movements and known aspects; and so, to us the Stillness means:

NO-THING"...

*I wonder IF **creation comes from "Nothingness"?***

I wonder then: ***Where does nothingness come from?***

What IF:

There never was a beginning nor an end, and so ALL life is a spiral, a circle within a circle; and we are *Divine living Beings within a Being, within a Being, within that which we refer to as: God/Goddess, Great Spirit, Creator*

However, ***IF:*** something begins, it must have an end...or so we THINK; but,

What IF: that is not so?

Then how can we comprehend God/Goddess, Creator, or even ourselves?

We ask:

"*I wonder* how All could be? Well...

What IF:

There ***WAS a beginning***, but that beginning grew so fast, and tunneled so long, that it met itself; and that until we travel its long path, returning to the point of Nothingness, we can never grasp the concept, never understand

What "*The Beginning*" truly is?

What IF:

Our journey here, viewing and experiencing the variety of other paths of seeking, is a preparing of our selves for:

The "KNOWING" of the Nothingness?

What IF:

It is in the **No-thing-ness** that we meet ourselves?

What IF:

It is in the ***Nothingness*** and the *meeting of self* that we meet *God/Goddess*?

And... *What IF:*

God/Goddess is that whirling pulsating energy?

And... *What IF:*

That Energy that appears to be full of Dark and empty Nothingness is actually but an illusion our minds have erected, (created), until we are prepared to "*see*" further through the "*darkness*", and look *not* ***FOR*** the darkness, but rather ***BEYOND*** the darkness, *beyond* the "dark holes" and seek the Light... search for it?

What IF:

Just beyond the dark there *is Light*, and the dark is also light, but light vibrating at a lower or higher speed then most can sense at this point of their evolving into conscience awareness? So...

I wonder IF:

We would "embrace" "our dark", our fears, and our chaos; then, look for the "Light" within it, *within us and within others*;

I wonder IF:

We'd find a brighter light then the "dark" we first felt , seen, and expected?

What IF:

That darkness was but *the vacuum that sucks the light forward,* and when we receive it, it but means and is "saying": ***"I am the Bringer of Light! Will you accept me? Will you look BEYOND what YOU THINK you have, and what YOU THINK you have NOT? Will YOU look beyond what YOU Think/bring? Will YOU look WITHIN ME and see that I am within the Dark AND WITHIN the Light; that BOTH are also:***

"WITHIN YOU and WITHIN ALL CREATION?"

ALL IS CREATION!

And, creation

IS

ALL!

I wonder IF:

We'll never understand, never KNOW, and never "see"

The Great Mystery, The Great Spirit, God/Goddess,

Until We understand "The Black Dark Nothingness",

And thus,

Understand Ourselves?

I wonder...

What IF:

THIS, *IS* TRUTH?

Written: April 16, 1999

✡ ✡

BEFORE YOU CAN KNOW WHAT LOVE
IS,
YOU MUST FIRST KNOW WHAT LOVE
IS
NOT...

"To Know Love"
Message Author 'heard', telepathy,
From a Spirit Messenger
1991

"Out of chaos, comes order…"
…First chaos, then order…?

"It is the pulse of The Spiral of Life"

---The Author
February 18, 2011

"We, The Children of The Morning Star:
The Children of Light,
Will rise up with the birth of the 'new' Earth.
Join us by raising the vibration of the 'strings' within you! Allow them to 'play their chords' that activates the Light Body to 'dancing you up to' :
The Fifth World of Light!"

The Children of The Morning Star
And The Author
July 07, 2011

*

LIFE

* ************************* *

IS MORE

* ***************** *

THEN

WHAT YOU SEE

****

*

"CLOSE YOUR EYES..."

"WHAT DO YOU SEE?"

"Ponder This"
The Author, July 04, 2011

READER'S OWN IN-SPIRED WRITINGS

****

READER'S OWN IN-SPIRED WRITINGS

****

CHAPTER FIVE

"CLOSER TO *THAT* WHICH WE ARE..."

"CLOSER TO WHO AND WHAT WE ARE"

If thou canst comprehend these things, thou knowest enough...

---William St. Clair, Scotland

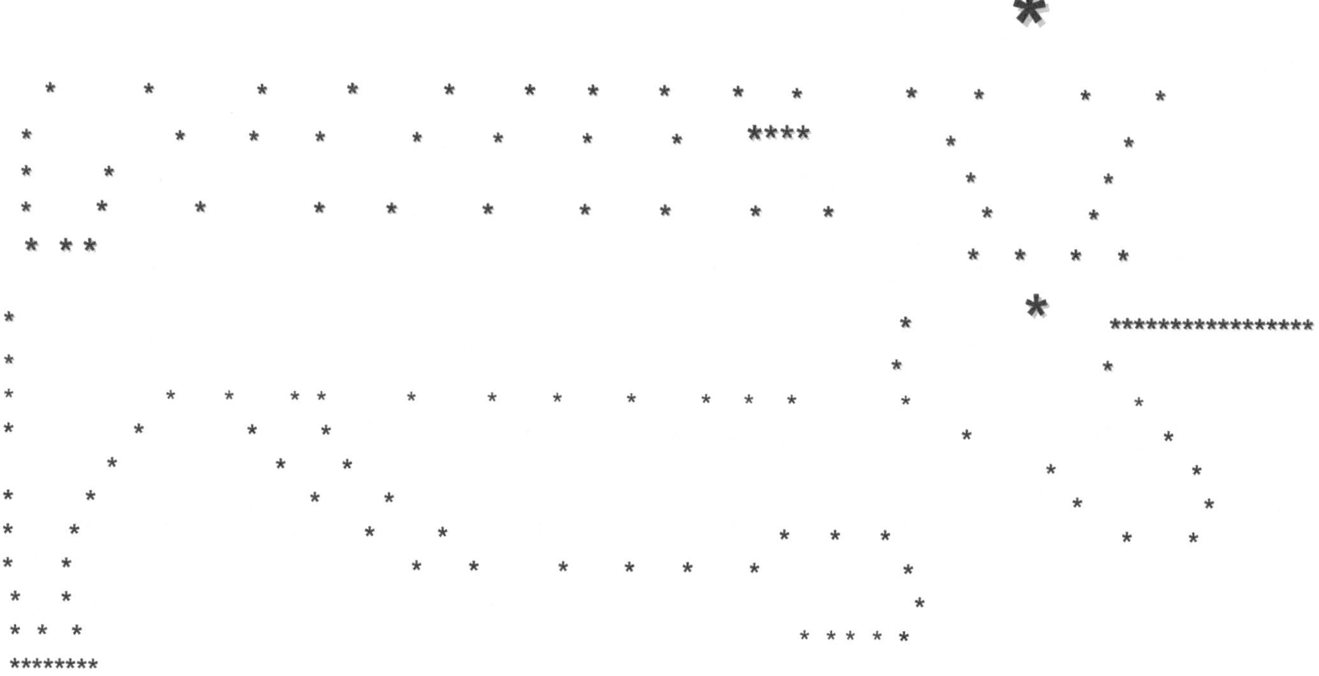

Great Spirit, Great Spirit, My Grandfather,
all over the earth the faces of living things are alike...
look upon these faces without number and with
children in their arms, that they may face the winds
and walk the good road to the day of quiet.

Black Elk (1863-1950)-Oglala Sioux Holy man

Wind in my "Shadow,
Rain in my "Hair",
Voices of my Ancestors,
Wisdom to share---

On the "Wings of an Eagle",
In the "Cry of the Hawk",
Comes the path of the "Dreamer",
In the Silence of "The walk"---

"THE PATH OF THE DREAMER"

The Author, Dr. R. Lowery-Hawk
Written: 1994

White winds and yellow breezes---
Green sands and purple hazes---
Dark blue trees, and red bright leaves---
Orange Sun, and golden Moon spun---

✡ ✡

Creatures walked and stalked the night,
Things were big and bright in sight ---
During the day the creatures did play,
Soft Magical Dreams, their music did sway ---
"The Storm Dragons" sailed across the Silvery Sky,
"The Rainbow Unicorns" closely followed by---
"The Knobes" peeked out their pointed capped heads,
"The Elves" danced merrily in their flowerbeds---
"The Faeries" watched in invisible content,
For all life here was pleasantly spent---
"The Faeries arrows" never left their bow,
Cause all God's Children were friends, not foe---
And, in this greenery,
Together all did trod,
Over and through,
The valley of:

"THE DRAGON OF DRODD"

"Dragon of Drodd", the Valley's "Mascot",
Belonged to a Magical Loving lot---
His scales were purple and violet too,
He was winged with black and royal blue---
His emotion could change the colors they say,
And he could fool you in his camouflaged play---

** ___ ___ **

He was fat and fiery too,
And his eyes slanted red,
With a glow starry blue---
He blew smoke, and he breathed fire,
But to do only good was his heart's desire---
The Earth shook when he did trod,
Oh! That big Lovable "Dragon of Drodd"!
When he flew across the velvety sky,
The land was darkened to all passengers by---
"The Storm Dragons" bid him "adieu",
They only wished to enjoy peace too---
"Dragon of Drodd" kept the land
Happy and content,
With the promises and Love 'he' lent---
And so...
When one wishes to travel,
to the "Land of content",
And, with his life,
Sweet Harmony be spent---
Let his mind softly drift, not nod
"The Magical Valley" of:

THE DRAGON OF DRODD"...

"THE DRAGON OF DRODD"
Written: Saturday, September 18, 1987

The outline of the stone is round, having no end and no beginning; like the power of the stone it is endless. The stone is perfect of its kind and is the work of nature, no artificial means being used in shaping it.

Outwardly it is not beautiful, but its structure is solid, like a solid house in one may safely dwell.

---Chased-by-Bears (1843-1915) Santee-Yanktonai Sioux

Stones

("Tones")

Every thing that is, IS alive!

It is alive with molecules, atoms, protons, electrons, etc. These particles are so small we cannot detect them with our physical eyes. (Man has, however, invented machines that can.) These particles move, and the *"Something"* that propels them to move, is referred to as Energy or Light. Vibrations produce Energy/Light. Even color has vibration, therefore Energy/Light. With this in mind, it shouldn't be difficult to believe that stones also then vibrate and are a form of Light and energy. Remember also, that living particles of Light and vibration are making up this creation that we refer to as:

STONE.

EVERY VIBRATION HAS FREGRENCIES.

These frequencies vibrate at different levels of speed. Some at low points; some at high points; and all with the probability of moving from one point to another. Stones have their purpose in creation. Their vibrations "feed" the earth energy, and so their energy goes into our feet and into all we eat, therefore feeding into US! Because different Stones contain different colors and vibrations, and both have vibrations and are energy containing different properties, each then produces a different effective energy/vibration. People throughout time have felt these frequencies, and so have made use of Stones for a variety of reasons and purposes. The lodestone may have been the stone that first brought about this awareness. (The lodestone has magnetic properties.) To name just a few of the uses of Stones: to promote healing; to raise one's energy level; to aid one's focus; and to bring about calmness. Basically, stones were and are being use to assist ANY need physically or spiritually. Stones have been used as tools ever since mankind discovered, through observing, and sensing, that humans and all life, including the Stones, were producing different frequencies. They began to notice, from the stones, the sensations of frequencies higher then the frequencies they were currently themselves vibrating; yet, frequencies that they might need, at different points of time in their life.

...The more we become aware of the energies around us, the more we can develop our own intuitive nature which will then enable us to come closer to
the awareness of WHAT we are,
And WHO we are becoming...

Written: 2002

"This is the story of how the "Stone People"
Came to be in the Sky and upon the Earth..."

"In the long ago time, the 'Stone people' could 'talk' with man and woman, and...with all other life... In those long ago times, and now as well, the Stones held the people's memories. In fact, they kept the memories of Mother Earth and of all that lived in her and upon her. Why, they even held the memories of the Stars and the Heavens! In fact... they came from the Stars!

Now 'listen' while I begin the story
Of how the Stone People came to be...

Long, long ago, in the beginning, before time, there was a 'Great Serpent' 'coiled up and around its Self'; for the 'Serpent' was very, very 'cold', very, very alone, and, in the dark'. Pretty soon the 'cold' got to be too cold! Being wrapped up in a 'coiled ball around her-Self' for so long, began to cause her to cramp with discomfort...and so, the 'Great Serpent' decided to 'stretch her-Self out' so that she could feel comfort. Slowly her 'tail' began to unwind, passing her 'face'. The 'Great Serpent' saw for the first 'time' her own 'tail'! She watched it as it 'uncoiled away from her, as she stretched', until she could no longer see it. "What? Who was that?!" she asked out loud to her-Self. Then she thought excitingly, and spoke out loud: "I'm not alone any more! 'The Great Serpent' then said to her-Self: "I must find who-ever that was and bring her back to keep me company!" She did not know the 'tail' was part of her, for she did not know she had a 'tail'! So the 'Great Serpent' moved her 'head' in the 'direction' she had seen the 'tail' go. But no matter how hard she tried, she could not find 'who or/and what' had passed her. Soon she stopped her searching, relaxed and told her-Self: "I will rest a bit and soon 'she' will become lonely too and then will come looking for *me*. When I have rested, if 'she' has not found me, I shall go and look for 'her again" But before long, 'Serpent' again became very cold, and so she again began to 'coil her body around her-Self'. That's when she saw 'her'! (Of course it was her own 'tail', but she did not know that yet). 'Serpent' quickly dashed out to reach this mysterious *something*! Finally she 'grasped it with her mouth'! "Ouch!" she cried out, for she had 'bitten her own tail'! This of course caused her discomfort and surprise, so she released her 'tail'! When she had released her 'tail' and yelled "ouch!" it had caused her to jerk her body and her 'head'; and so her 'tail' then swung back in the opposite direction. "Where did she go?" 'Serpent' shouted in question. "I must find my 'new friend'! And way she went in the other 'direction' in search of her new 'friend'. This searching and 'grasping of her tail', and then releasing it caused so much twisting and turning and heat, that soon Little Particles of Bright Light were flying off the 'Great Serpent'. Away the sparks flew! "Oh! What is this?!" the 'Serpent' asked herself in surprise. She stopped her spinning and looked at all the tiny Sparks of Light. "Come see this!" she shouted to her 'friend'. When 'she' did not come, 'Serpent' began her chase again. When she became tired, she rested, and when cold, she coiled herself back up. After she rested she would again see her 'tail' and so would again begin the chase. She would 'grasp her tail in her mouth', and then when she would 'feel her mouth on her tail', and in either surprise or discomfort, she would release it, spinning the other way. By doing this, her movements again created Sparks-of-Light...particles in the darkened sky! Pretty soon, all these movements and all the opening of her 'mouth' caused her to 'fill up with the Light' she was creating; so much Light that she had to open her 'mouth' wide to 'push the Light out of her belly'! Out came the Light in the form of an 'egg'! An 'Egg' of Great Bright Light! The 'Egg' was brighter and larger then the Little Sparks of Light' her body had first been throwing off. (This bright 'Egg-Light' was all the little sparks of Light gathered together inside the 'Great Serpent's belly', but now all together as one bright 'Egg-of-Light'.) 'Serpent' looked at the 'Egg' in surprise then she said out loud to her Self: "I'm truly not alone anymore!" And then...she 'smiled'...The tiny sparks saw the large Light in the shape of an egg, and so they too did not feel so frightened and so alone. They observed and saw that the 'egg-Light' resembled them because it too shone and was round, and so they felt comforted. Soon all the tiny sparks of Light began to gather around the 'Egg' to keep warm and to feel comforted in the dark. They felt 'fed' by this brighter, warmer Light.

«THOSE SPARKS OF LIGHT BECAME OUR FIRST GALAXY OF STARS. THE LARGER LIGHT BECAME OUR FIRST SUN, OUR FIRST SOLAR SYSTEM...OUR NIGHT SKY.»

Soon all of the 'little' sparks began to 'laugh' with joy like a small child, for they were indeed just 'children' at this point in 'time'. Their 'laughter' caused them to sparkle and their 'bellies' to move around and around, 'jiggling' inside. Soon they too were 'throwing of' 'little'' new particles of 'Light-Sparks', just like their 'Mother' did: the 'Great Serpent'. Now there were even more Light' in the sky! The great "Serpent" would open her 'mouth' wide every time she would view this new world around her. She would chase her 'friend', (her 'tail') one way and then the other trying to share her joy, the wonder, and the beauty she now was experiencing. She wanted to share it with all that she could 'see', all that now existed... not just her 'tail', (that part of her she could not always see, but could sometimes glimpse and touch for a very short while.) Each time the 'Great Serpent' would open her 'mouth' in wonder, Light would enter; and each time her 'belly' 'tickled' she would 'laugh'. Every time she 'laughed', out would come an 'Egg-Shaped-Ball-of-Light'!

**"THIS WAS THE WAY THE STARS AND THE GALAXIES WERE FORMED.

But, as the 'Little-Sparks-of-Light' grew 'older', they began to get 'tired' quicker then they use to, and so they didn't move around as much as they use to, nor shine as sparkly nor as hot and bright, as when they were first created. Because of this, they did not 'laugh' and 'giggle' as much as they use to, and so the light inside them begin to dim... (They too like 'The Great Serpent' had allowed some Light inside them). Because they did not move much any more nor 'laugh' as much, the older Lights joyful 'giggles' of 'Lights' inside them slowed down also. Soon these older Stars-Lights grew so 'tired' that they could not 'open their 'mouths' wide' enough so to let out the collective 'Little-Lights' that were inside their 'bellies'... and so, because those 'Lights' inside the older Stars began to slow down, they began to become dense---they became heavy and hard. They became: matter! Yet, since there were so many of them gathered inside the older Stars, they were then able to help the older Stars. They could feel what the older Star, that they were in, was feeling, and so, (for the time being) they soon began to willingly forget about their own personal desires of moving out and becoming a 'Great Egg-Ball of Light'---to become a Great Sun... They 'said' to one another: "There will be many other 'Eggs-of Light' to help the 'Little-Ones-of-Light' that are outside this older Star-Light that we are now inside of; but who will help this older Star we are in if we do not?" And so, they 'pulled' together and they did the very best they could to help keep the older Star comfortable and 'alive'. They also wanted to offer their Light for warmth to the older Star and they wanted to keep it from being 'lonely'. The 'Little-Sparks-o-Light' would 'talk' to the older Star, and they would also 'giggle' for that older Star-Light. When eventually, the older Star would begin to break apart, the many Little Stars inside would work together to help hold the older Star together...and in the Heavens.

Soon the 'Little Sparks/Stars' inside learned to communicate with not only the older Star they were in, but also the Stars and all the Light-Life outside of the older Star. All the Stars, all around, then began to help the older Stars and the Stars within the older Stars that were growing too 'tired' and too 'weary'. The older Stars then, after a time, began their own rhythm of movement that was a slower, denser movement. This movement then created another form of life and its many life forms. Movement of any kind created a life of some kind. The older Stars soon cooled their hot, heated Bright Light and became softer, cooler, slower Light-of-Life. The older Stars then became what we today call: Planets.

Soon, because all the Stars helped one another, the 'Great Serpent' also helped, and so became strong, remaining in the sky, always creating more 'Baby sparks of Light'; then releasing more 'Eggs-of-Light' into the Universe. Now with all this help, the Planets began to create new life of a different kind, yet of the same substance from within them, springing forth upon them. The Planets and the ever-changing Universe now worked *together* to help keep them and *all* life going and becoming more expressions of it-Self. Some forms of life we humans cannot see with our physical eyes, but some of us just know that life is there... and life that is there is living and sharing life with one another and with *ALL* of us! Some of us can feel that life...

THE GREAT 'SERPENT' BECAME KNOWN AS: 'EMERGING LIFE': "THE LITTLE STAR LIGHTS INSIDE OF THE OLDER STARS'— THE PLANETS—BECAME KNOWN ON EARTH AS: MINERALS, ROCKS/STONES: TONES OF VIBRATING SOUNDS/MUSIC AND THE 'RECORD KEEPERS' OF MEMORIES OF THE BEGINNING OF THE PLANETS EXISTENSE. WE, OF THE OLD WAYS, KNOW THEM AS:

'THE STONE PEOPLE!'

"And, that is the story of how the 'Stone people' came to be in the Sky and here on our Mother Planet: Earth; and since the 'Stone People' have been since the beginning of time, (plus, *they remember*), they then are also the 'Record Keepers-of-The-Heavens', and so then, *ALL life*...that means also: you and I...*all* people! And, of course, our Loving and Dear Precious:

"Mother Earth..."

...When you next see a Stone, a Rock or a Mineral of any kind, hold it in the palm of your hand. Try to still your thoughts. Feel. Try to feel it 'giggle'. Some times it feels tingly, sometimes it feels fuzzy or warm, and sometimes *ALL* of these things. If you 'listen' from *inside yourself*, if you 'listen with your heart', and send them Loving feelings and thoughts, you might 'hear' or 'feel' them 'giggle'! If you do this, *AND*, you *believe*, they, and the Stars,

MIGHT even 'talk' with you...

WRITTEN: 2002

* *

*** I heard them in the breathe ***
* Of the wind; *
* While branches moved, *
* And leaves descend--- *
While stillness gave sound,
With peace profound---

They spoke to me,
In voice of song;
Tunes that were me,
In Soul belong---

It was their voice,
And yet,
It was part of me,
As I felt their presence,

In the voice,
In the wind,
Of the trees---
** **
*** ***

"The voice in the wind of the trees"
WRITTEN: 1984

*

BACK TO THE HOME OF THE HEART-WAY

* *

Many "voices" pulsate in my veins:
Whispers, offering secrets of where they've been---
I feel them rather then hear them,
Starting as restlessness;
Some forgotten need,
Grasping a breath,
In me,
Wanting to be reborn
And free----
The blood that runs through my "Mother"
"Calls" the loudest and the strongest---
My "Mother" is green and yielding,
She "carries me upon her back";
She supports my every move, and my every need----
My "Mother's" "blood" runs green and runs "red",
Calling to me to return to "The Green-Way"; "The Red-Way";
The "Heart-Way",
To return to:

THE NATURAL WAY Of LIFE—

Other "bloods" have merged with mine:
Some unseen power,
Pulling and calling ALL "bloods" to merge as one---
These are my Ancestor's "voices",
Meshed in MY blood:
THEIR blood that runs in MY veins---
Am I then my Ancestors?
So, WHO am I?
Who are *YOU*?
Who were *THEY*?
...Each moving in me,
Through me,
"Calling" and "whispering" the Truth-Way;
Each THEIR way:
The way of THEIR blood,
Their blood that makes up MINE!

✡ ✡

...But, it is my "red blood" and my "green blood" that calls to me the strongest
Telling me to "come back" :
"HOME"

✡ ✡ ✡ ✡

✡ ✡ ✡ ✡ ✡

So, *WHICH* do I *want to be*?
Are we *ALL* then: "*WANNA-BE-S*"?
Are we not then "innocent" and perhaps "possessed"
Of and by our Ancestor's blood?

* *

By their "voices" propelling us ever onward and back to
The same "Home", the "only Home":
That place that only the "Heart" knows;
That place among the Stars,
By way of our Green "Mother";
Back to her "womb",
And back to her "Heart",
To understand,
And then find our way,
Our special way,
Back to:

✡

"THE HOME OF":
"THE HEART-WAY"

Written: February 14, 1999
11:55-12:03 A.M.

Do not forget the plant "Clan-dom"s.

They are your friends and companions of life. They feed you, they heal you they comfort you, and so much more!

They keep you alive!

Have you taken a few moments from your busy life style to ponder what this "clan-dom" gives to you and all life here on this planet? They give you *much*! They give and give and give AND give!

Have you connected with them today? Have you asked them? **What** have you asked? What ***should*** you ask? Have you *thanked them*?

Who are *they*?

...Who are you?

We use to know...

The Author,
July, 11, 2011

You have noticed that everything an Indian does is in a circle, and that is because the Power of the World always works in circles, and everything tries to be round...
The sky is round, and I have heard that the earth is round like a ball, and so are all the stars. The wind, in its greatest power, whirls. Birds make their nests in circles, for theirs is the same religion as ours...
Even the seasons form a great circle in their changing, and always come back again to where they were. The life of a is a circle from childhood to childhood, and so it is in everything where power moves.

Black Elk (1863-1950)
Oglala Sioux Holy man

We are ALL related.
The animals are our brothers and sisters, as are the plants and all life known and unknown.

We are more then we seem...
We are sharing this dream...

We are all of eternity......

---The Author
July 8, 2012, 12:14 A.M.

Infinite worlds appear and
Disappear in the vast expanse
Of my own consciousness,
Like motes of dust dancing
In a Heaven of Light---

___ Ancient Vedic Saying

READER'S OWN IN-SPIRED WRITINGS

****

READER'S OWN IN-SPIRED WRITINGS

****

CHAPTER SIX

"STIRRING THE STARS"

Be ye therefore wise as Serpents,
And harmless as Doves...

----Matthew 10:16, The Christian Bible

THE GREAT MYSTERY

(GREAT MYSTERY COMMUNING WITH THE AUTHOR)

AUTHOR: "I feel you are giving me a message...are you telling me the Coyote is a symbol of innocence, not *just* trickery? "

GREAT MYSTERY: "Correct. The symbol of Coyote is many things, and so it represents many things. It is symbolic of the many trials and lessons learned, and needing learned, in life.

I call upon each of my children to play the part of the 'Coyote' at some point in their life. Coyote, for example, can represent innocence. Many think of innocence as being without experience, knowledge or the knowing of right from wrong. They compare innocence then with stagnation or ignorance. Yet Innocence can open the 'door' to trickery, and trickery can some times open the 'door' to Truth (painfully or wisely). Truth then opens the 'door' to ME. Coyote also represents the 'fool'. The 'fool' then seems foolishly innocent and ignorant, catching the unexpected, (including Self) in the Truth of that moment, and the truth of themselves. This also leaves one vulnerable to others and to one's Self. This is a test for all involved. It brings about the assembling of the 'missing parts' of you, we: US! It brings about:

"COMPLETNESS"

Written:
December 16, 2002
2:37 P.M.

The White Moth flutters,
Awakening in the Night—
She's driven by her memories,
Of the comfort in the Light—

The drive she is following,
Creates a Spiraling Dance—
One that chances The Fire,
Of the Light's beckoning trance—

Yet, onward she flutters,
Steadfast in her goal—
Sensing Truth in the "Fire",
Innate knowing "secrets of the old"—

"The White Moth"
Written: February 20, 2011
1:50 a. m.

"THE BUTTERFLY"

MAY NOT UNDERSTAND THE "WORM",
YET, FROM THE "WORM" IT CAME...

WORM IT WAS;
BUTTERFLY
IT

IS...

Change leads us forward into

"Becoming"...

The Author
WRITTEN: 1999

Alone
at night,
In my bedchamber am I.
I wait for what?
I know not why.
But it calls to me,
Though, no one else can hear.
It whispers on the wind,
And, carries to my ears.
My bedchamber curtains dance,
In breeze do play,

* *

While whispers like music,
In still of night do sway.
There is something familiar,
In their whispering sound,
Something more dear, more real,
Then before ever found.
There is a feeling,
That awakes in me,
A yearning, a longing,
A need to be free.
Free to be what?
I can'st not say,
But, at night,
Its beckoning
breath,
Takes me away.
It seems I sleep,
But, yet, I wake,
And, strange things,
Strange memories I take.
And in these misty moments
Of dreams once spent,
I live a life of Magical,
Familiar Content…
I see strange
Small folks,
They dance with me.
I feel small hands,
I see a great tree.
I smell scents from
The forest deep;
I talk with
The plants
Even though
I sleep.
But,
Do I sleep,
when at day-break I wake,
With leaves decorating my gown,
And, my blanket my cape..?

"NIGHT WALKER"
PUBISHED IN: AMERICAN POETRY
A Book of Anthologies (Contest winner)
WRITTEN: September 16, 1989, 5:00 P.M.

"DANCING THE STARS DOWN"

In the long ago time, before the forgotten time, there was a movement that began ALL movements. It stirred the wind to blow, the grass to sway, and the birds to wake up! The movement stirred *ALL* life to wake up and about. In those days of the long ago time, everyone paid attention to the movements. They taught the young, that they could hear life's language spoken on the wind, when they slowed themselves down... and so, the people had learned to listen to the wind... Those who had learned well soon began to notice that the wind had moved inside them. Perhaps it was always there, but it wasn't until they had listened to the movements around them that they began to notice the movements inside of themselves...which reminded them of the wind. It was THEN,

They began to dance...

Their dances imitated the wind and all that they now were aware of. There was the dance of the motion of a child's first stirrings from the "sleep" of the mother's womb. There was the dance of the motion of the "Great Fear" of the beasts and the unknown that lurked somewhere in the dark beyond where their fire's light reached. There was the dance of the movement of the water as it came forth from the sky, washing them clean and then joining with the earth to form lakes, rivers, oceans, and creek beds...water coming forth to form what appeared to them to be the Earth Mother's veins full of life: water! Water then to them became earth's blood. Earth's blood gave her and them life! Its fluid offered drink to a "thirsty" people, to a thirsty world. There then became a dance of water, becoming the dance of earth. It was then that they took notice of the sky, the sun, the moon, and the constellations. It was then they became aware of the "camp fires" in the sky; and, it was then they began wondering if there were others like themselves in the heavens! They wondered if there were people in the sky like themselves, sitting and perhaps dancing, around fires.

Their dances became the movements of life.

The people found themselves studying the "fires" in the sky more and more; and so noticed that the stars seemed to dance in the heavens. The stars' twinkling lights soon became the people's dance also. And so, they built a central dancing fire in the center of their camp, and there they danced around the fire, imitating with their dancing, the heavens and their constellations, the earth and her elements...They then had created a dance for all they became aware of. They were observing and imitating life around them, but also the life above them: the life in the heavens! The people notice all life had movement and so, they imitated those movements, creating ceremony and dance! The people had observed their fires on earth, then the heavenly "fires" "dancing" above. They had observed the movements of the planets, the movements of the wind, the waters, the earth, and the many life forms upon the earth...and, they had observed the canopy of the star-fires in the sky. They then contemplated upon these things and so began to realize there was a "fire inside them" like the ones above them. They eventually began to become aware that life

above reflected below and then all around, finding its way back to the heavens. The fire they had seen on earth now represented to them *ALL* of life! The fire represented to them the life inside of them, above them, and inside of ALL things! To them the life force inside them was like the fire of the stars above them. To "bring" the stars beauty and light to them, they had built "star-fires" on earth by way of building central fires in their villages. They then danced to the right, around the fire, imaging and imitating the star's/planets seemly movements around the much brighter, hotter and larger star: the sun! They moved around the fire, spinning, imaging themselves being part of all the cosmos' movements above them; and then spinning in the other direction to the left, representing the movements of all the life on their Earth Mother. They spun counter cock-wise to also represent the light and life that mirroring back, returning to Earth. Their dances became for them the movements of life; calming them, pleasing them, focusing them, feeding them, warming them, celebrating and healing them, and their Earth Mother. Their *
*dancing*became*their*inspirations,*motivation,*and*their*commun-ication...their communion with themselves, their Creator, Earth Mother and, with all the various other life forms.

THEY DANCED AND THEY DANCE,

and...

"They danced the stars down",

Knowing and feeling the Star Particles, as, their very own...

DANCING THE STARS DOWN"
WRITTEN: December 17, 2002

*
*
*
*
* *
✡ ✡

Journey of The Soul,

Is a wayward path
Its course winds around obstacles
And collisions of fear; making stops at Indecisions
And false illusions formed
From deep "valleys of sorrows"...
*****The Soul's journey is: "three wise women spinning And weaving",*****
"Threading webbing, the fibers Of yesterdays"; blending the "tears" of Forgotten Dreams
Into the "Golden Tapestry" of the Future-Child; taking each of their Hope-Dreams,
Of their pass sorrows and then alchemizing them into New beat; into a new
***Tomorrow's Child**...*
The journey of the Soul is a wayward path, ever circling,
Ever spiraling to beyond "Tomorrows" and "yesterdays";
Resting on imaginations and "dreams"; "webbing paths"
Of: coming AND be-coming...
Ever becoming...

The Soul's journey IS: "Three wise men",
"Stretching", yearning, bending, and turning: the "Golden Tapestry of time".
Balancing and "Stretching" all that the "Dream-Child" can "dream";
Then, "wrapping" it all into "bundles" of: "I can's", "I am's", and, "I will's"...
Aw, yes, Soul Journeyers, Tomorrow's Child,
******Light your "flame" and "dance" your Soul's "Dance", least you forget:******
Your "Heart's Song" and,
The way its path,
*** "Sings" ***
✡✡✡✡✡✡✡✡

WRITTEN AND READ:
December 1996
In Santa Rosa California, on the radio show: La Rosa

Wisdom:

"The Beast and The Beauty"

You must be made empty to become full.
You must enter the void to be in the All.
It is through experience one gains stillness.
It is through stillness one gains knowledge.
It is through misunderstandings
One arrives at understanding.
It is through understanding
One arrives at wisdom.
And it is through knowledge *and*
understanding one *earns* wisdom!
Release the "Wild",
Allowing it to run free,
YET, "tame the Beast"...

****

* When one thing comes,
So also, comes the opposite---its counterpart.
Learn to: "Pull them together" in harmony.

---

* "When wisdom moves forth first, moving like the "Serpent", *before* the knowledge and understanding, (a knowing) thereby and therein, shall you "dance with the stars", and reach the:

'Golden Wisdom Gate' of:
The 'Heavens of Heavens'...

If your heart is pure, and your faith true and calm, all knowledge of under standing and wisdom then shall unfold before you...

"Seduce" the opposite into a blending of harmonious oneness then one can become a master of one's Self and one's life, thus, live in blessed harmony, balance, and beauty with prosperity in *all* forms of "needs' in one's existence. The human ego—"The Beast"—reacts to stressful stimuli and fear, and, when undisciplined, can send its words and thoughts out to create turmoil/chaos, conflict and confusion to Self, and to others. It would be a great disturbance for anyone, if allowed to rule; but particularly so for that one who has "awakened" and so, created a activated "power" source within their Self. Wakening power is a gift AND, a responsibility! Knowledge and wisdom comes with a "price"; for it bestows "power" that propels the balancing forces to manifest and to return more quickly. This also means returning to YOU! If a dark intent is made, even with or without an action, the affect will seek to return again to the sender: the cause; for this is the natural law of universal balancing for order. The repercussion that comes to change the impure and unjust intention could then be severe in its disturbance. It is through knowledge and under-standing, experiencing and empathy, compassion and wisdom, one evolves and ascends. And so **we** shall!

BEAUSE:
"The Beauty seeks Beauty",
"The Beast *finds* the Beauty",
Then, *TOGETHER:*
"The Beast and The Beauty"
Seeks BEAUTY and THE BEAST...
Finding:
BEAUTY!

WRITTEN: 1999

"A Wise Dreamer"

(Our personal world forming)

*Our personal world is formed by our thoughts, our perceptions, conceptions, our actions, and, our re-actions. This is not only a concept difficult for many to believe, but also to understand and to accept as Truth... Yet, with close observation of one's life, thoughts, and actions, one can find a pattern, and thus, see this truth. Our thoughts bring to us our life's challenges, our lessons, and our experiences; therefore, our "growth". All of this creates our "personal world" thus, OUR "reality"---creates what WE conceive and perceive to be "real"; and so then, becomes our personal "truth". To change our personal---perceived---"world", (and the collectively perceived "world" all of us together live in, and are creating) into a much happier, peaceful, and better world, we need to change our destructive thinking, and speaking, and our actions and our re-actions. To do so, one should pause several times a day to get in touch with one's thoughts. Are you thinking habitual negative thoughts, and self talk? Pause and then concentrate on, and "feel", the peace and Love within. This will help you to think positive and healthy thoughts towards self, others, and the kind of life one seeks and desires. This is also beneficial for the world as a whole. These pauses and meditations will train, condition, and discipline the mind to a good and healthy way of thinking, so creating that which one desires and feels they need for survival and a happy, healthy, Loving, and balanced life. From doing this, one's "world" shall change, following the thoughts and the feelings that are deeply believed and held to be real and true. We "dream" our personal "world" into existence. All our individual and personal "dreaming", our believes and our thinking, create thought-forms that mass and mesh together as a collective "dream", thus, creating our "world" of our collective **real**ity...our **real**ization/belief of **Real**. This then brings about much in ways of creation, which can create joy, but also includes Chaos and its challenges, thus: lessons. As those who do not hold majority of collective beliefs to be their "truths" try to hold on to their own beliefs, (thus, going "against the grain"---going against the masses,) chaos and confusion then is "stirred up". We then must be faithful and calm in ourselves, in Love, in good, in the Creator, and, in maintaining our faith and our peace. The chaos then shall find no place to call "home", and thus, find no place to ad-heed to. The uncomfortable chaos merely signals change leading into balance and synchronistical order. Change is movement. Movement is life. Life must move or become stagnated: polluted, toxic, unhealthy and diseased, deformed ---distorted! Our exploring life's positives enable us to co-create and harmonize not only a better environment in which to live, but also to make a better human out of us. If you wish to change the way your life IS, then change your "dream", or it shall change you! The "Dream" (the world you are believing, thus, creating), if unchanged, shall remain as it is, and possibly even worsen in its compliment to urge you to hold true to your "Heart-*

of-Heart's" truth. If your thinking goes against the good of the whole of life, chaos then shall also come to steer you away from the destructive patterns of your thinking and believing; your actions and your reactions. Discernment is important here, for chaos comes in many "languages"---many messages, for many reasons. All creation IS moving towards becoming more, and better. Therefore, look for the positive reasons for the chaotic energy and happenings. Discipline yourself in these positive ways and habits and you shall "awaken in the dream", and then "dream" (imagine and create) a truer world for yourself and, for others. This truer world is one of ever turning Circle of Love, balance and unit: caring for one another.

Awaken and co-create:

"THE DANCE OF BECOMING"

****

"YOU ARE 'THE DREAMER',
'THE DREAMER THAT DREAMS'---
ALL THAT YOU SEE,
IS TO YOU, WHAT IT SEEMS---

YOU MAKE IT, YOU SHAPE IT,
YOU CREATE AS YOU GO---
YOU ARE 'THE DREAMER',
YOU CREATE...YOU DREAMED IT SO"---

So, "Dream", feel, think, believe, and energize into being-ness that which is good and Divine for you, for others, and for ALL creation as a whole. "Feed" the "Dream" several times a day with good and joyous feelings, and thoughts. "Feed" it with Love Energy! Wish, desire, hope, believe, and create---manifest---neither disharmony nor hurtful and negative "some-things", for any-one or any-thing. If you do, the "Dream" shall turn to/on YOU. It shall do this because you shall then be THIS! You are a part of the whole of creation! Every thing IS connected and depends upon every-thing for existence. When you "Dream", you are the creator of that "Dream", creating with the power of the Higher Source that has given you free will and free choice. Since you are also a part of ALL THAT IS, your "Dream" then also comes back full circle to you, the "parent"---its Creator---the creator of the "Dream" you have given "birth" to.

A WISE "DREAMER"
Written: September 12, 1999

"THE COYOTE'S RUN"

+++++ +++++

\+ The "web" was already spun +

+++ +++

For the Coyotes had run---
And, from them you could not stray,
For your request had cast the day---

And so,

The tests were about to begin,
From front to back,
And back again---

++ It would spin them around, and inside out, ++
\+ Then take them to, where they are about--- +
It would throw them back, to side to side,
Bringing forth, what they tried to hide---
And so, the Coyotes ran that night,
To test the Spirit's request for sight—
Its only when one faces their dark,
One is able to walk that path they embark---
Their battles are themselves they fight,
Locked within and out of sight---

And, so they'll be tricked into truth,
But, to find the mysteries they seek,
It's their *own* dark they must defeat---
The way then that it's revealed,
Is through tests of illusions seeming real---
And, for many, that is done
By way of:
"The Coyote's Run"

WRITTEN: Monday, December 16, 2002 @ 2:35 P.M.

"MYSTICAL SMOKEY LOOKING GLASS"

Mystical looking glass,
Smokey reflections of me,
Viewing many dimensions,
Moving in the "sea"---
Smokey looking glass,
"Veils" I put over me,
Yet images
Made known,
In other's reflections I see---
If in you, I see,
What I then do not like,
In me I then see,

What I let leave my sight---
Reflections of me,
Everywhere I see,
Cause ever time I look,
Myself,
Reflects back to me---
Teach me my True Self,
And...
Similarities in others
I see---

WRITTEN:
September 1994

"BATTLES AND LATERALS",
"TATTLERS AND TALES",
"JUMPERS AND STUMPERS",
PARADISE AND HELL—

COMBINED TOGETHER
"THEY RING A GROWTH BELL",
SAYING: "ALL ARE EXPERIENCES,
AND ALL IS WELL"—

THE AUTHOR
July 11, 2011
11:30 P. M.

"BITS OF WISDOM"

✡ ✡

* DARKNESS FADES,
"WHEN YOU FOCUS LIGHT UPON IT"

*WHEN ONE ONLY LOOKS AT THE FRONT OF THINGS,
"ONE LOOSES WHAT IS BEHIND IT"

*ROUGH ROADS,
"CONDITIONS THE WALK"

* YOU CAN DUNK YOUR "DONUTS",
"BUT NEVER LOOSE SIGHT OF THEM"

SMILE!

** **

* *

* *

WRITTEN: October 27, 2002, Sunday

She thought she knew him...
But his face was not clear---

The rain had come often and hard this year, making it difficult to remain the same. Could he too have changed? It wasn't so much the outer image that was altering, but rather, the inner Light, reflecting outward a difference. The rain drew out and cleared away the toxins shed from the "old stuff" which was not serving the pure Light; and so it brought a healing crises and a confuse-ment, signaling a need for rest; as if one was cocooning, awaiting the new brilliant Light;

awaiting their re-birth...

Indeed

The metamorphosis of:
"A Child of Pure Love & Light"!

"REBIRTH"
THE AUTHOR
JULY 12, 2011, 12:10 A.M.

KNOW,
IT *IS* THE
MOMENT...

---THE AUTHOR
August 03, 2011

"AND THE STARS SAW,"
"AND THE SEA KNEW..."

---The Author
Feb, 12, 2011

Infinite worlds all around us like stars
And their Star dust,
Mirroring THAT within us.
'Stir the stars' to stir the truths...
'Stir the memories'...

---Author
August 03, 2011

READER'S OWN IN-SPIRED WRITINGS

****

READER'S OWN IN-SPIRED WRITINGS

****

CHAPTER SEVEN

"CALLING THE SACRED"

Wisdom is the principle thing,
therefore get wisdom,
with all thy getting,
get understanding...

----Proverbs 4:7: Christian Bible

"What part of you should I call to?
Your mind? Your liver
What part of you should I call to?
WHICH is in need of Love?
Should I prepare a "bed" and,
Warm it with the "Bed Warmer"?
Should I put it to sleep?
Aw, but wouldn't THAT be a comfort?
REALLY..?
* *

Where then, 'around the "corner' do *YOU* stay?
Do you 'lurk in the shadows' there?
Behind the large door'?
Or, is it the 'dark closet' you hide in?
Do I need to seek to find?
Is it the game of hide and seek, **you seek *your-Self*?**
For how long?
Pass noon? Midnight? Pass that which you call: TIME?
Oh, Dear One, I shall 'play your game'...
...UNTIL YOU TIRE...
I will move where you move. As you flow, I shall flow.
THIS, ***Dear One,*** I shall do and do,
Until you ***slow down*** so you can see ***me*** ..
Until you ***KNOW*** that I, which you run from,
Is but ***your own 'shadow'...***
I am your shadow only because you run,
And therefore, cast me aside and outward
To follow you, rather then 'dancing' WITH you...
'I am your Dance Partner'.
'TAG! You're 'IT'!
NOW, *find ME!*
'Dancer'
" Dance WITH me"...

"THE GREAT MYSTERY"
(Message Received for all people)
WRITTEN: September 1995

The "Fire" is being stirred,
Over-there, long ago;
The story is being gathered,
Forever to be told—

People are awaiting,
Nothing is amiss;
They're gathering the "story",
Of life's golden bliss—

The secret is buried
Not far from where you stand;
It lies In your Heart,
Its "key" is in the land—

The Fire-Key Story"
WRITTEN;
February 15, 1999, 2:01 A.M. Monday

Somewhere in the distance, far away,

There could be heard the rhythmic sounds of Tribal Drums. They, the three of them, who had camped and sat at a campfire that night, went silent and still as they listened to the unexpected sound, in a place where drums could not be found...

A warm wind began to stir, moving across a cold night; stirring gentle some-where's and lost dreams, while the three 'held time in their hand'. Tears broke forth and slid from each of their eyes, as joy swelled up in their hearts. They could not explain the affects that night; they only knew what after, remained...

The drums that sounded from far away had brought them back to an ancient call: a place they knew they were from... After that night, each of their lives would be changed, for their Spirits would soar for something more. Because, that night, when the drums had beat from somewhere far away, 'a sleeping mystery' descended upon the campers three. The sound stirred awake their memories of long, long, ago. There came that night, an ancient "call" that beckoned to that which lied deep within. It called out to the dormant ancient cell-memories *that were "listening and waiting": they awaited the* human will's readiness, *so that they might* again *"dance" to the tune of where they and all mankind have been,*

and...

"Where they are going to"...

"TRIBAL DRUMS"
Written: December 05, 2002

✡

✡

✡

"I AM THE HEART FREE-ER"...

I COME TO THOSE WHOSE PRAYERS HAVE ECHOED IN THE CHAMBERS OF THEIR SOULS, LONG AGO; AND CRY WEAK AND MUFFLED; AWAITING UNTIL THOSE TINY MUFFLED CRIES ARE BRAVE ENOUGH TO BREAK FORTH, CLEAR, AND CALL THROUGH THE NIGHT OF: "THE DARK OF THEIR SOULS".

I COME TO THOSE IN SORROW; IN CHAMBERS DARK AND LONELY, WHERE THEIR "ECHOES OF TEARS" NEVER CAN RESONATE ANYWHERE BUT INSIDE; LOCKED WITHIN THEIR OWN "SELF-WALLS" THEY, THEMSELVES, HAVE ERECTED...

WHEN THESE "WOUNDED-SOULS" REACH THEIR "BOTTOM", "TOUCH, AND THEN CHOOSE TO RISE AGAIN, WHOLE" AND REMOVE THEIR "MASKS", GIVING UP THEIR "BOUNCING BACK AND FORTH IN LOST CORRIPDORS"; IT IS *THEN* "A HOLE IS TORN IN THE MANY VEILS" THAT THEY CONCEALED THEIR TENDER HEART WITH. IT IS *THEN* THAT THEIR "CRIES" ARE SENT TO THE *SPHERES*; AND IT IS *THEN* THAT THEIR ECHOES CALL TO THE *CHERUBIM* AND TO *THE ONES ON EARTH WHO HAVE CHOOSEN TO WALK THE EARTH AGAIN* SO TO *DOCTOR* HER, (MOTHER EARTH) AND HELP HEAL THE SOULS OF THOSE WHO HAVE **FORGOTTEN** THE "DANCE,

DUE TO:

"THEIR OWN HEART WOUNDS..."

"MESSAGE GIVEN TO THE AUTHOR"
FOR ALL PEOPLE
FROM THE GREAT MYSTERY-CREATOR:
WRITTEN: May 21, 1999

"Is it sorrow that stirs me 'awake'?
Or is it the thought of joy that's
'Awakening' me to the searching
Of my 'True Heart'?
Both have lead me here..."

—*The Author*
February 08, 2011

THERE COMES UPON THE EARTH A DESCENTION...

Like a mist it shall cover its face---
At that time, the four directions shall meet---
With the continuous line's movement,
There shall the center be one---
The center then shall move,
Becoming a circle within a circle,
Within a circle, within a circle, within---
At that time, there will be four breaths
upon the face of the Earth,
Becoming into four movements, extended into seven:
One above, one below, one beside;
And, one beside the beside, all around---
One in back, one in front; and one within ALL---
The Mist is a Song;
The Song becomes The Dance;
The Dance Becomes...
All is Becoming---
ALL is coming!
Prepare a place...

* *

Prepare a place *within*,
To prepare a place without;
"Dance " the DANCE, Sing the SONG,
Sing! Sing:
"Spirit to Spirit, *One* Song belongs;
One mind, one Spirit
One dance, one song---
one... one... one... one..!

\+ *"11:11"* +

"MESSAGE GIVEN TO THE AUTHOR":
(FOR ALL PEOPLE FROM GREAT MYSTERY-CREATOR)
WRITTEN: May 04, 1994

*MESSAGE THAT IMMEDIATELY FOLLOWED THE PREVIOUS ONE:

The "Mother" is "*pregnant*" and about to give "*birth*". *You, (the chosen people) are the "midwives"*. The *prophecies* are unfolding and being fulfilled. The White Calf Buffalo is about to be born. Soul families, Soul mates, are coming-together, Gathering into "clusters": communities/circles. *Women*! Dance the vibrations up to assist the *"laboring of the birthing"*; Sing the dimensions into form! *People*! "light" your fires! Light your fires on the outside, but on the inside as well. Re-kindle them!

Women! Assist the *men* in the *re-awakening and rising of the feminine* so to *awaken* the *Family Ancient-Star-Ancestral-Memories, and your Earth Mother's memories*. Join hands and danced for and with the "Song" that gives way into the "*birth*". "She": "The Space", is *collapsing*, and "He": "The Time", is following her. Time and Space afterwards then shall rise up quickly! They will be renewed and not the same as what you are accustomed to in this space-time-continuum. *Sia and Aion* then, *shall join*, united in the *Sacred Union/Marriage: Two becoming one in sing-u-larity. Two Becoming One to Become:*

"THE ONE"

(The "IS")

THE WHITE CALF BUFFALO: MIRACLE, WAS BORN THREE MONTHS LATER IN WISCONSIN

"Channeled" through the Author
Written: May 04, 1994 Thursday

"THOSE WHO ARE WAR-LIKE
WILL RESIST ME,
FOR I BRING TO THEM:
'THE BOUGHS OF LOVE'---

When the wind cast its last breath,
There, shall you find your destruction---
When the sea sends its last spray,
There, you shall remain---

For, (because) eons of time,
When the Forefathers walked,
You spun your 'web',
And 'threw it' to the 'wind'---

The wind was your shelter, your provider,
And, your friend;
Yet, you stood not forthright and strong,
While able to 'bend as she blew' ---

Now, the time has come upon you:
Which way shall ***YOU*** 'blow'?
Will you leave your 'wares of destruction'?
Or 'carry them upon your back'?

The 'road' is long,
and the 'road' is hard,
To those who have lost,
their 'sap', their 'pull'---

'Travel light', as you meet the 'night',
For over 'the bridge of tomorrow',
Shall you roam;
And, over that tomorrow,
Shall you find your way...
'Home'...

Peace be with you...
"Ohm-eh-shah-naw"...
(Message from the Great Spirit- **"Message for *all* to "wake up")**
WRITTEN: Saturday August 28, 1993

Sacred Prayer-Enchantment

****

"Ku! My people, my Ancient Ancestors! Hear me!
Gha! I am here! I feel your heart beat! See me! "

" I still breathe your breath!"

"Oh, Ancient Ones, Old Ones of The Mountains, do not leave us! To do so would scatter the foot steps of the Silent Ones. The Silent Ones dwell in the quiet places, there where only memories stay. These are the 'Record-Keepers': the thought forms that hold our world together. Their 'records' are the memories of the Ancient Ones that spoke to our Ancestors.

Oh, Ancient Ones of the Sacred Mountains! You call to us! Thousands of us hear with the instinct to move towards that feeling of 'call'; Most not completely aware of what they move towards---

Oh, Sacred Mountains! Your power medicine is that which holds the energy fields of life; that holds what we hold as real here, in an embrace of what we call reality: our world of Mother Earth--- All across the land energy pulsating, is dissipating, yet, in your center it pulses the strongest---

It is there in your 'Heart' I'll find my truth, dance with my Ancestors, and gather 'the gift of records' that you wish to bestow upon me, and upon those whose Heart still beats, and still "breaths", with the breath and the Heart of:

'THE GREEN MOTHER.'

'Ku! My people! My Ancient Ancestors! Hear me!
Gna! I am here! I feel your Heart beat!
See me! I still 'breathe' your breath! "

WRITTEN:
February 15, 1999, 12:30 A.M.

The people gathered,

While above the Heavens grew dark...

There was a rumbling somewhere far off in the distance. The aging medicine man looked up, focusing his attention for several moments upon the darkening sky. His aging but wise eyes then slowly traveled to those of the old medicine woman. Their eyes met and held for a time, words in the silence of their minds passing between them. Slowly the medicine woman bent her thin, aging knees, stooping low to the Earth. She then pressed her aging dark hands flat on the Earth; closing her eyes as she directed her senses to her hands and through them to the Mother Earth. The people were nervous, whispering among them selves... But, one had been carefully observing the medicine people, and so had signaled to the people for silence. Overhead, the Sun was quickly being covered by a 'black shield', as 'a blanket of angry clouds' began to rapidly move across the sky. The medicine woman slowly stood up, gracefully, in spite of her advancing years. She then quickly, raised her arms and hands straight over her head! Simultaneously, looking upwards towards the Heavens! Instantly, the darkened sky 'screamed out' as a deafening roll of thunder announced it self! At that precise moment, the medicine man quickly raised both of his aging hands over his head! With that, lightening awoke, danced, and laced the darkening sky, gathering with it: POWER! *Within seconds, a large bolt of lightening made contact with the earth, not more then fifty feet away from the frightened people, sending all the hair on their bodies and head straight up while their insides seem to tingle and hum with an electrical surge! The people were frightened, some braver and more trusting then others, yet, even they trembled before the power and the mystery of the unknown! The children and the more frightened adults huddled together, clutching one another close! The children cried, as did many adults! People had dropped to the Earth Mother/Grand-mother, praying, trying to shut out their fears! But, at that moment, the large lightning bolt had joined the Earth, sending a vibration throughout her! She then... began to quake... The movement started gently, then gained speed, quickly gathering strength, trying to 'shake off' all the offending forces from within her, and, upon her weary 'back'! The people cried out, looking frantically for a way to escape, but...there was none...*

The observer: their head-leader, motioned for the people to remain where they were and to have faith with calm. The medicine people's chanting, which had begun when the lightning bolt had struck, never ceased but continued uninterrupted by the activities around them. It was important that the people remain calm and where they were; crucial that they 'stand still and keep a calm and single eye.' 'The sun was no more…captured' by: "The Shadower"!

The sky and the earth were black. The people wept; the earth shook; and, the chanting increased in speed and tempo…The ancient medicine man and ancient medicine woman were with the Spirits, joining with the sky and the earth: becoming ONE ***with them; Moving with them; breathing with them…***

"Grand Mother Earth's warning, long ago"
WRITTEN: March 1998

If you seek The Brilliant Light of God,
You must be willing to ‘dance through the “fire”.

----*The Author*
February 16,
Wednesday, 2011

In "The Shadow" did I "dance",
"Hand in hand";
Swirled and swirl,
Unhappy and resisting;
In the beginning,
Not knowing
That my "Dance Partner"
Held the "secret to life",
To "my freedom",
And,
To my universal goal..."

"THE SHADOW DANCER"
Written: 1995

✡

ᏄᏚᏇᎷ ᏋᎱᎥᎷᏳ ᎷᎱᎬᏚᏣᎥᏳᎱᎬ ᏠᏈᏳᏋ ᏳᏋᎱ ᎱᎥᎷᏳᏋᎬ ᏄᎷᎱᏅᏇᎱᏣᏯᏈᎱᎬ.
ᏳᏋᎱᎬᎱ ᎱᏣᎱᎷᏅᏄ ᏠᎥᏰᎱᎬ ᏯᏚᏣᏣᎱᏯᏳ ᏳᏚ ᏄᏚᏇᎷ ᏋᎱᎥᎷᏳ ᏳᏋᎱᏣ ᏳᏚ ᏄᏚᏇᎷ ᏰᎷᎥᎥᏣ

YOUR HEART RESONATES WITH THE EARTHS FREQUENCIES.
THESE ENERGY WAVES CONNECT TO YOUR HEART THEN TO YOUR BRAIN

You must "face and embrace"
Your "shadow",
If you are to know, so to understand:
"The Dance of Light".

"FACE THE SMOKEY SHADOW OF THE 'FIRE"

----The Author
Feb.12, 2011, 2:12 A.M. Saturday

CONNECT AND KEEP THE SACRED CIRCLE WITH THE EARTH MOTHER
ᏯᏚᏣᏣᎱᏯᏳ ᎥᏣᏫ ᏗᎱᎱᏢ ᏳᏋᎱ ᎬᎥᏯᎷᎱᏫ ᏯᏈᎷᏯᏢᎱ ᏠᏈᏳᏋ ᏳᏋᎱ ᎱᎥᎷᏳᏋ ᏜᏚᏳᏋᎱᎷ

They call me Aion...

I "play" with the "sands of time"...

I view them and then shift them as is needed for creations' "dance". If I move even one grain, I change creation's route to another one, and that movement creates ripples that dance out another way for everything. It would seem that I control the "dance", but I do not. I only "play" and watch as I "sing".

I love to "play" in the "sands", and my "songs" are a part of my "playing". My "songs" calm the "sands". I "sing" the songs of creation as I "play" in the "sands of time"... It is my "song" that guides the "sands" and calms the "dance" you are "dancing". If I do not "sing", and I shift the "sands", things will become chaotic because "a chaotic and confused ripple" will begin to move as I "shift the sands". This chaotic and confused ripple then gains speed and becomes "insane" with a chain re-action that quickly spreads. When that happens, I then must "dance"; and when I, Aion, "dance", time collapses to the degree of my "dancing". This "dancing" brings about purification, and that brings about the "death" of that which will not change as is needed when I had only "sung". If I "dance" faster, all that is not realized as a part of the whole of creation, and all that are unwilling to change for the love of the whole, will have to be re-cycled with the "dance", and so, spiraled away and into: re-creation. I love to "dance", but it saddens me when I have to "dance" *without* my "song". I am saddened because I know that the fast "dancing" will bring much discomfort and even great pain to many, for they will not understand. My heart is sad for I know that with all this "dancing"; Sia must endure all the effects.

Be prepared...

For if I, Aion, begin to "sing" while I "dance", Sia then....

***Shall* "Sing"**

THE DANCE OF AION – (AEON)"
WRITTEN: August 03, 2002

THE THUNDER DREAMERS AND
THE RETURN OF THE DRAGONS

The fire was built up high, for it would be a long night filled with stories. Stories were important to the people, for they were their link to themselves and their world, and the days and nights had grown too cold for much else. Everyone in the small village had gathered around the fire in the center of the village. They covered themselves with coats and blankets to keep away some of the bitter cold wind that seemed to have picked up after sun down. Many found logs to sit upon while others stood huddled close together for warmth.

The year was present time: 2011. A storyteller and teacher, and a stranger to them, had come offering stories. She, unknown to them, was a messenger of the creator of life, "riding the lightning of the thunder", carrying within her the stories and songs of the old one's knowledge and wisdom; stories and songs of the sacred and forgotten truths that had been lost to the people. The villagers did not know who she was. No one had seen nor heard of her before. She had simply walked in from the west as the sun set. They did not suspect in the least that this stranger among them carried within her these truths of life from the Ancient Ones of eons pass; for she presented herself simply, appearing as one of them, offering what seemed like merely a distraction from their discomforts. She was gentle, and spoke with a comforting melodic voice, appealing to their senses and their loneliness. She drew them like a flame beckoning to the "white moth" within them that longs for the light. This teller of truths, cloaked in stories, had been traveling for years to communities that she was divinely guided to go to. This small village, hidden in a remote area, just outside a large city, had been her next designation. She had traveled for months, bypassing other communities on the way. She had a mission, and she was steadfast and calm in her destiny's call of service. She naturally moved onward, her head held high with conviction of purpose, to fulfill that mission with a purpose that was she. She had arrived from the west, just as the sun had lowered itself over the distant hills, casting its last light in a spray of bright red.

She stood wrapped in a purplish blue cloak made from some unusual looking material that appeared light, but must have been warm for she never shivered nor seem to notice the bitter cold nor the howling wind. Rather, she stood among the gathering people serenely with a gentle loving smile, observing them, receiving imprints of them, "listen" to the vibrations of the conscious of the community as a whole, sensing its nature and need. She studied the people individually as well, allowing the stories to look through her spirit "eye" and choose the peoples they wish to belong with. This cold night, there was a great story-fire pulsated wildly within her, wanting to be set free to join with the people in it's serpentine dance of moving through them, so to enlighten their personal inter fires to: dancing "the hidden" awake. "Striking them" into remembering, as the telling-dance sings to them, moving, gyrating, developing and becoming…becoming their story… Their story was the story of the Thunder Dreamers, and the return of the Dragons: The Good-Medicine- Dragons.

A large dark cloud gathered as the storyteller exhaled the deep breath she had taken. She began to spin the currents of waters inside her, with the sacred wind-breath she took; stirring up and bringing forth the living story within. On her next breath she began the telling. The breath's current, like a loving and gentle wind, moved forth from her mouth in its birthing of a story. The "child": the story, moved over the people, embracing them and wrapping them in its spell bound gift of love. This, their story, began this way:

"In today's time, and the almost forgotten time, there was (and **IS***) a "Great Serpent" that lives in the center core of the Earth. At times, this great Earthen 'Serpent' sleeps; its breath softly moving within its body, lifting it gentle and smoothly…as it sleeps. During these times of rest, the Serpent stills, and quiets all that lives in and on the surface of the Earth Mother. All sleep or rest, reserving their life force until the Great Serpent awakes again and begins its movement towards moving upward and breaking from out of the Earth's core. When this happened, all life within and on the Earth moved also, joining in the Serpent's dance of awakening. The way it moved to the surface was: The Serpent moved around and around and side-to-side, gyrating, creating ripples in the earth and in those upon the earth. As it moved it gained strength until it reached the top, and with a great power and breath, it burst forth and through the Earth's womb, rising it's head up. Now, in the time of 'almost forgotten', there was a great power within some of the people on the surface of the Earth. They knew how to guide this power that is in the Earth, in her elements, and within their self, and, within all that existed on and within the Earth. It was a time of unity in confidence, truth and knowing. The people of long ago knew that the Great Earthen Serpent down under, would rise when the large bright, hot, Golden Sphere in the sky moved closer to them. They knew 'the breath that moves across the waters' on their world, the earth mother, would blow and awaken the Serpent. When this happened, they knew their dancing back of the Golden Sphere: The Sun, would begin bringing forth not only the Great Serpent beneath them, but also, the transformation of the Serpent, and of…themselves, along with ALL life that came forth from the Earth which they called: their mother or Grandmother. When this transformation occurred, the Great Serpent would bathe on a large s/tone, allowing the hot, yellow ball of light, which moved closer to earth, to transform it into an above protector of the people, for the people, the earth, and all 'children', all relations (life) that lives upon Mother Earth, and that which lives within her. The Great Serpent would transform into a creature with great wings…."*

The people listened; fascinated with the "dream" she was re-spinning in the matrix of Earth, above the Earth, and into and through the matrix of the people. As the storyteller had begun speaking the next five words of the story, a loud burst of thunder suddenly erupted from the sky, startling the people into a jump, and impulse to stand up and run. But the storyteller continued calmly with the story, without a pause in its beat, therefore, the words rolled on, meeting with the crash of lightning, just at the precise moment in the story where it was mentioned, just as the thunder had done. The people looked from her to the darken sky where the thunder and lightning had come forth moments ago. The storyteller continued on without a pause, as if it had not happened, holding her audience in her spell of words. The people calmed and settle again back on the ground, once more caught up in her melodic rhythm of words in the telling. These were those words she had spoken, that called the thunder and lightning to join the atmosphere, gifting power to and within the story: "A Great Being of Thunder (the thunder came forth at this moment in the story) would then come from the sky, upon a lightning bolt, (the lightning bolt came forth from the sky at this moment in the story) to complete the transformation. The winged Serpent would then rise and meet the Great Thunder Being, twirling and swirling, mating in a dance of power, bringing needed conditions to all upon and within Earth. Now, there were some among the people of old, who understood the winged Serpent and the Thunder Bird-Being. Because of this, the Dragon, the Serpent became, in its transformation, and the Thunder Bird, that the

Thunder Being became, would listen to these people. These people who were selected by the Giver of life and the spirits of the keepers of the balance and the records of earth, were able to get the Power Beings and the Dragon and Thunder Bird to come to their beckoning call and aid them in the protection of the people and their Earth Mother home. The Dragons, answering the medicine people's call, then became also, the Guardians of the Earth and all it's inhabitants. The other worlds of spirit trained and filled these selected people with love, empathy, knowledge, wisdom and understanding, giving them medicines, (gifts of abilities, knowledge, wisdom, understanding, and many other important and necessary gifts), along with empowerment and knowledge and wisdom of the applications of these gifts, along with the information that the above beings sent to them on rays of different light colors; each with their own vibration frequency and gifts. They, who received 'medicines', were referred to as: medicine people, people of different medicines, knowing what and when and how to apply them. They gifted these people with what was needed to survive in harmony, peace and unity of love…wellness, on this third note of crystallized-density-dimensional plane (world/planet), of existing vibrations (notes and tones) of sound and light. These chosen people, would watch, observe, and assist with the renewing and transforming of energies that needed cleansed and transformed continuously. These chosen people guarded and balanced life. These people who were chosen were also chosen due to their own choosing, and their willingness to go through the 'fire' of purification, facing their own 'demons', so to arrive at that point of capability and wisdom for receiving the gifts. They each were given a choice: to not go on or to go on with the light and the preparation they had been chosen for. They were chosen after many conditioning trials and lessons on many levels and layers of purification. And they were chosen due to their baring of the affects of the purification's drawing, and still choosing and desiring to continue on for the betterment of life, with love rather then anger, hate, revenge, and violence. The purification is one of releasing one's own 'demons' that keeps them in oppression and bondage to untruths, fears and the surrounding dark that blinds and binds them, keeping them from the love light of truth that awakens them to all that ***IS;*** *which opens them to the love they are:* ***IS****. They have stood up to that which is always releasing, or, TRYING to release from them and all others, including the planet. The 'darkness', (disease-ment/toxins) having been released, then draws more of its kind to be transformed. Yet, these 'choosen ones' withstood, keeping their journey onward in the intention and purpose of unselfish love. Their love was for not only their self, but for All that* ***IS****, was, and will ever become. These chosen were given a choice to either use their newly earned gifts, for the light of love and harmonic betterment of ALL of creation, as well as the earth they now called home, and for the welfare of the race of human beings…the real people, or to chose to be one who brings about the trials and the darken material for practicing transformation and creating, to the people and the world. The trials, if not understood, and one not trained in the knowing of the dark's spirits and how and why it/they are, would bring an un-harnessed and uncontrolled power of darkness from an untrained people that would bring upon imbalance and disruptions of destruction, therefore, much in the ways of scattered energy and confusement, resulting in great and painful sensations of discomfort or lost of love. It would push the entire conscious of this world back into a forgetfulness of who they really are, and send them into a 'sleep-walk of the lost'. This place would be the 'hell-place of NOT-KNOW', the place of the ' lost Child of light'; Lost to what and who they are, shrouding them in blinded despair because of this lost of: knowing love. Choosing to bring challenges could, however, condition, and teach the* *people, through experience, and eventually wearing them down to the point of their deciding to chose to seek more light and love in their life and their world; and thus, rise up out of the "mucked waters" of stagnated creating they'd been doing; and then, thru their discomfort and despair, chose to create order out of chaos, rather then be the creator of chaos that is out of order with things. Chaos out of order gives chaos as a angry gift of energy- material to others to confuse or hurt them. Doing that only sends the same back to the sender/doer, yet, ten times stronger. Choosing to transform chaos and the imbalances of light into a river of flowing abundant love, teaching one the power that lives within the dark and the light, can, and is meant, to create and transform into the natural heart beat of life: balanced love flow to all that* **IS.** *Chaos is meant to be utilized for creation. It is a trainer and allows you to experience change and its affects. It is meant to let you try out the truth of creating, showing you that you can master co-creating with God-Goddess (higher Giver of Life), in the beauty way of love and blessings for all existence as one body, one heart, one mind. Experiencing the dark also allows you to decide what 'stuff' is not serving the divine balanced love and good of and for all life as a whole, and what does. It will teach you, through its affects on you, others, and life.*

The "Dragon" began to bring forth more "Dragons" by mating with the "Thunder Bird". These new Dragons were half Dragon and half Thunder Bird. Together they guarded and protected the Earth. But then, a disharmonic wave of foreign Beings entered the Earth's atmosphere, veiling it and the people from the mantle of Creator God's light, separating the Goddess from the God. These bringers of "dark" had Dragons and Thunderers of their own making, of their own kind, their own likeness. They were in the likeness and the image of their makers. Their intentions were dark and frozen chaos. They blocked out the light of one of the many hearts of God...that great, golden, warm and sometimes hot, sphere in the sky: the Sun of the Earth, thus separating the Goddess from the God. The "Knowing people" of the gifted medicine-powers, knew these Darkened Ones, their Dragons, their Thunderers, and their **Dark** *Thunder Dreamers, wanted to take over the Earth and create disharmony, so to use that disturbed imbalanced light to feed upon, and then vomit it back out as thick vibrations so to stifle, control and manipulate that vibration into a denser world they could thrive in. The medicine people of the bright light of love and peace, also knew these dark invaders sought to capture and change their loving Dragons of the Blessed Bright Light into serving them by manipulating the elements here on earth so to "catch the Power Beings of Earth's sky, thunder and lightning" in their blackened Serpent's mouth, (the wormhole of their world), devouring them. They wanted to prime and manipulate the forces of power on Earth to change their original directions and instructions of aiding the light on this planet to ones of aiding the Dark Lords and their light energy sucking needs instead. Those with the medicine gifts of light, love, sound and the powers of many other gifts of light from the light Giver of love and peace and beauty, knew they had to protect the Dragons of Earth, so to have a means of preserving the future of Earth and all upon her and within her. They had to send the Dragons to another dimension, another world where anything or anyone of an impure heart could not see them nor find them. The Dragons had given birth to more special Dragons. The people of medicine had to protect the baby Dragons as well, so they could grow up and have the chance to gain more strength and power, while they watched and observed the ways of the darkness that was beginning to descend upon Earth. This would help them to understand this enemy and learn the wisdom of how to disperse it and send it back to where it came from, and/or transform it into light that serves creation of a higher nature of light. They knew that the Thunders* *and the Thunder Bird/Beings of Earth served to allow the best for Earth and it inhabitants. It was their inborn nature because it was what the giver of life created them for and allowed them to become. So, the medicine people knew they would help hide and protect the Dragons. The medicine people then, sent the Dragons to another higher frequency; a higher vibrating level of Earth: the upper world, that exists beyond the vision and knowing of those on earth who had yet to earn the gift of seeing and hearing or even awareness of that existence. Those that had earned those gifts were those who sent them there. They sent them to ' the place of the light of the world'. The place where eyes cannot see, and ears cannot hear, and darkness cannot find. Only those with a pure heart opened to the source of love, and light, and have earned the 'Keys to the Heavens/ the universe', can, and are allowed to see them and hear them; thus, one day when it is their 'time,' call them forth to again ride the currents of love here on Mother Earth. To one day again, protect her and all her children, giving them hope again, and the assurance of continuous life.*

The Thunder Beings sent their "lightning" into some of the medicine people, and into the Earth Mother, creating a Thunder People connected to the 'Father Sky' and the 'Mother Earth'. These Thunder People could travel in their dreams, entering their own sub-conscience, super-conscious, and also other's dreams, and, other worlds, planes/dimensions of existence. These Dream Walkers could then use their gifted abilities of bringing forth the light for transformation through their hands, their eyes, their voice and their mind, in these places where darkness and demons tried to spread their darkness and hunger. These medicine people, these 'Children of Light', these 'Children of the Stars', could also invoke the thunder and lightning to come at their command by calling out its name. The Thunder and the Lightning were allies of these selected Thunder Medicine People, gifting these Thunder Dreamers with the gift of even a mightier power of this planet's energy and light whenever their own gift of bringing forth the light for transforming seemed to fail or not be strong enough to transform some of the most vicious dark beings they would encounter. The Thunder and the Lightning would come to the strong sound of their name being invoked for the need of their power. The Thunder and the Lightning would then transfer their power of light to the Medicine People---the Thunder-Dreamers, at the moment the Thunder and the Lightning came, announcing their arrival in sound (the Thunder) and in sight (the Lightning). The Medicine People then could transform the darkest of inities that they came across, be it in this world and their so called awake state or in the other dimensional worlds in their sleep-dream state of body rest. The dark inities came in many images, such as beasts or demons, or even in humanoid forms, that tried to destroy them. When, and if, these dark beings came too close to the Dragons or to the spreading of darkness to their world, and to other worlds, (which could destroy their world, and other worlds as well), these Medicine People could then fight them. They could seek them out and destroy them with the help of the Giver of life, who was from beyond even their understanding and sight, the Thunder Beings, Mother Earth, and the light beings of love, from other worlds. They could harness and use the light from the Thunder and the Lightning for the purpose of power so to protect. They were Spirit Warriors of light, transformers, to protect the earth, the people, and all life here and on other worlds. These Medicine People would chant words that rolled out of their mouth, sounding sometimes like gibberish, building up energy of light in them, then when they felt 'filled up' they would release it through their hand to the Thunder and the Lightning, calling them, invoking them, in a strong voice, calling out their name in the force of a command. The Thunder and the Lightning, would then gift the power of light through the sound of thunder, and the sight of lightning, when and as each were called forth. They came because they knew it was what they were created to do: give electrical energy and sound for the use of what was needed to keep this planet and all she produces functioning at a united cooperative motion and flow. These actions, this purpose and gifting, they were created for, and it brought them to life more fully! It brought balance and protection so that life, and them, could continue to give life, bringing forth more life. The lightning was needed for Mother Earth. The Lightning acted as a mate, meeting with the Earth, uniting, and joining with her; stimulating her to life and sending vibrations, like shock waves, down inside her, stimulating her to quickening and bringing forth life. They are partners. All things created have a purpose. All things were created to give to all things, coming back to all things. It is a circle of life. All things are meant to be in synch, for all things balance one another and bring about well being and love. All needs All. All mirrors All. All becomes….ALL.

'The Dragons' have now gained enough knowledge, wisdom and understanding, by their observing and conserving of energy, and from their observation and the learning about life where they are, and here on Earth. The 'baby Dragons' have grown up. They, along with the adult 'Dragons', have observed and learned from the dark time's affects on life and people here, and also the affects of the third dimensional vibrations of this plane of existence upon all that are here. They have learned many things, over these many hundreds of years concerning the darkness and imbalance brought upon the earth, of how to wisely be able to transform and return again to this earth plane, out of the dream plane of the other world that exists somewhere between the worlds. The Thunder Dreamers on Earth have helped clear the way. Send then gratitude from your Heart-Of-Heart's Love Center. They have cleared the Earth enough for the 'Dragons' to return to earth. Stand fast! For they have begun to awaken! The Thunder Dreamers are gaining power again, for they too were put to sleep for protection while the 'Dragons' drew from them some of the power they gave. It was to still the time into a calm before the storm of the 'Dragons'. It was to allow the ones from the other worlds of Light, sometimes referred to as Star Beings/People, and sometimes referred to as Angels, to come to earth on a gentler wave of Light, color, and sound, to plant 'seeds' of understanding and wisdom for the knowledge that they were bringing to the people of earth. The Thunder Dreamers were 'awake' and at their most power while their human flesh 'slept' in this dream-time (Earth-third dimensional plane); but they were 'awake' only in those other worlds other then Earth. They fought darkness in other dimensional worlds, training during the dreamtime while their human body rest (Slept.) on earth. They trained and were taught, awaiting the time to 'awaken' in these human bodies so to be able to better access and assist this third dimensional world dream time, fully 'awake'. After many years, The Thunder Dreamers are 'awakening' into more power, returning, along with the 'Thunder Beings' and their 'Thunder Birds', bringing with them the 'Dragons' of old. 'The Dragons' are calling to the Thunder Dreamers, the Star People, and all Children of the Light who are walking among you, under 'disguise' as people with non, or little, knowledge, and wisdom; 'disguised' as people with little or no gifts of medicine power, so as not to draw great attention to them before they are most needed. These Thunder Dreamers, Star Beings/People, and other Children of Light, have been trained in other worlds unseen and unheard by you, and are preparing for this time of ***Becoming****, and* ***their coming to this planet. They are here and are still comin****g! Coming for* ***the becoming of a new era****. An 'awakening' of* ***IS****!*

The past and the future are now!

The Dragons are 'awakening'! The Thunderers and the Thunder Dreamers of Thunder and Lightning, and the other Children of the Stars: The Children of Light, are being activated to 'awaken' to who they are and to their purpose and mission, thereby assessing their gifts of power! 'The Great Serpent' from the Celestials of the 'Ever-Rest' is watching, and its 'mouth is opening'. The 'Sleeping Serpent' is being 'awakened' from her 'sleep' within the Earth; breathing stronger breathes, quickening, to burst forth; rising her 'head' to meet the call..."

The voice of the woman began to rise in volume and strength, building and noticeably electrifying the air around them.

"BEHOLD THE *GUARDIANS!*
BEHOLD THE POWER WITHIN!
THE DRAGONS ARE COMING!
AND THE EARTH SHALL *SING!*
THE DRAGONS ARE COMING!

AND LIFE SHALL:

THUNDER DANCE!"

The messenger, who delivered the story, had given them no name to call her. It was hers to keep, along with its power. She stood motionless and silent before them, after having completed ***'their'*** *story. The villagers remained silent and stilled, speechless with awe and wonder. They were locked motionless and silent, as if by magic, in the power of the story, this story that was NOW their story. No one moved nor spoke, so absorbed in the wonder of it were they. The story "Seeds" were planted, being nurtured by contemplation, bringing the feelings of the Light and Sound of what it all meant. The "seeds" were being nurtured with the "Light and Water" of life from emotions brought forth from the rhymic telling. The "Seeds" within the story that had been gifted and lovingly deposited within the people; nurturing them with Love's multi-dimensional truths of Light;* ***awakening their encoded Divine DNA with the truths of life and who they truly are****, and, what they are* ***meant to remember****. These "Seeds" they needed so they could "grow" into the beautiful "Flower" they each are, so they then might become the "Fruit" with the "Seeds" of Light inside them; for the enlightenment of their many worlds within them, and the many worlds all around them and beyond; and then, share them with others.*

The story, having been told and given its life to live on in others, meant her mission here had been accomplished. A bright and beautiful aura began to pulse and come forth from her heart moving all around her. It danced and shimmered all around her in colors not seen ***yet*** *on this world. She then slowly, and silently, turned, her head held high, facing the east, and then, walked out of the village and into the dark night. As she did, Thunder and Lightning followed, and the Stars brightened in the darkened sky....*

Written by the Author's Star Higher Self
February 21, 2011,
3:45 A.M., Monday

It is in change we may meet sorrow—
If we accept and learn to flow with change,
We can learn and flow with tomorrow,
And then...peace shall follow—

-----The Author
July 01, 2012- In the Afternoon

WHEN EVERY HEART BEATS,
WITH THE ONE HEART BEAT,
IN THE SAME RHYTHM;
IT IS THEN ALL SHALL RETURN TO:
THE ORIGINAL CONDITION…
RETURN,
TO THAT,
WHICH WE SEEK…

"THE ONE SONG"
The Author,
WRITTEN: 2002

Take heed of your own Inner Fire: it is the Fire of the Divine:

Remember...

It is sometimes more important to *listen,*

Not just to *what is* being said,

But to what's *not* being said...

***

"Listen to the "in-betweens".

Listen,

With your "Heart"...

---THE AUTHOR
WRITTEN:
Saturday, November 20, 1999
8:30 A.M.

The Dragon ,The Seraphim, our Bearers of the Divine Fire of Purification....

✡ IS means a variety of things. ✡

✡ IS also means: NOW, ✡

Being in the present moment, being aware; being present and focusing on NOW for the life you want for you and your world. Time is an illusion. Time and space are collapsing. The Pass and the future are Now! Life for the future begins in the present moment.: the one-ness! You create; and your being present and aware will give you more joy, knowledge, and understanding. You then can create a harmonious and loving existence for yourself and for your world. The feminine principle of the Creator does that: it loves and *creates*; it opens you to understanding and wisdom. Combine with the supreme intelligence it brings about perfected growth, harmony and continuality. This feminine principle *is* WISDOM! She has been referred to as: The Shekina! Many also call her: the Holy Spirit. She exists in the now moment and IS! The m ale and the female principles of creation are balancing and creating the song of the One. Life is dancing to that vibration! The future is being created by what we do, feel, think and say, *And*, do not do, feel, and say, here in the IS moment. All life IS and it *is* happening now! IS means:

"MANY THINGS", that *ARE*.

(As this book has been conveying to you)

When you grasp its truths you then shall be in the KNOW... You will be aligned with the Shekinah: The Divine Feminine, Connecting, and embracing you with the Great Mystery in the "IS-NESS"... IS isThe Divine Feminine; the creating element; the era of the higher-frequency of light for manifesting new creation. Is-ness then also means: The Divine Feminine joining with the Divine Masculine, together, stating that they form truth and present-tense singularity: One unit of existence; thereby, creating together, the present moment...

* Make your *IS*-NESS count for the *betterment* of *all* life, for you are co-creating the future. We are *all* creating the world we are now living in, and the future world we *shall* live in. Create with Compassion, Peace, Joy and Love; for it patterns the world you wish to live in, and the person you wish to *Be*. Our world, our experiences will *Be* what we create in the *IS* moment. We have now interred into the era of *IS*. It means the presence of the quickening in the birthing of a new Earth; manifesting in the now! The feminine nature of

God has descended and birthing (Ascending)*a new world of: peace; love; compassion; healing; and, all beauty from a higher vibration. The relations of the four directions, the four races, are returning. They are coming together, bringing the wisdom and truth they have learned, and been given, from and of, the Creator and Earth.

Lets join together in this "Dance of *IS*".

It is:

'THE DANCE OF BECOMING'...

In the Spirit of Peace, Light, Love and Unity,

The Author,
Dr. R. Lowery-Hawk
July 05, 2011

IS: The I AM:
The WE in The I:
Of The I of The ONE...

MAY THE "IS" BE WITH YOU. BE (COME) THE BE IN THE NOW.
NOW BE!

"SET YOUR SPIRIT TO DANCING!"

Dance a dance, for the stars above.
Dance a dance, for the stars below (within).
Dance a little dance, for the stars of Love----

Dance a dance; they are watching, true.
Dance a dance, even a little dance,
Dance a dance, for all, and for you----

Dance a dance, for the stars above.
Dance a dance, for the stars below (within).
Dance a dance, for the stars of the "Dove"----

Dance a dance, they are watching you, above,
Dance a dance; they are waiting for you.
Dance a dance, even a little dance, for Love----

Dance a dance for the stars and their kind,
Dance a dance, for they are among you,
Dance a little dance, for now is the "time"----

Dance! Dance! They are watching, true!
They are waiting
THEY'RE WAITING, FOR ***YOU!***

(Patiently they wait...are YOU ready?)
...Are you ready for the power of Love? THEN:
'DANCE' YOUR 'LITTLE DANCE' FOR LOVE...!
...***Become:*** 'THE DANCE'...

The Author,
February 19, 2011, Saturday

"Keep your eyes on the stars, And your heart mindful of the Earth"

THE AUTHOR
August 03, 2011
Wednesday

"Be not forgetful to entertain strangers:
For thereby some have entertained Angels unaware ...

— Hebrews 13:2: The Christian Bible

"REMEMBER YOUR COMPASSION"

CHANT:

FORGIVE AND LOVE...
Hey ya, hey ya, hey ya, hey ho!
Hey Ya, ya hey ya, hey ya, ya hey, hey ho!
Sha nay, my tomorrow; ben nay my sorrow;

Shalome, Shalome, peace I follow---

Ohm Nay Ohm, Padre Ohm Nay,

Ohm Ma, Ohm Ra--

Ma Tri Mu, Ma Tri Ma, Ma Tri Ra,

Ma Tri Ohm---

Ra tri Ma; Ye Sa Le Du---

Ra Ma, Ma Ra

Hu---

Author
April 26 & July 02,,2012
Thursday----Monday

READER'S OWN IN-SPIRED WRITINGS

****

READER'S OWN IN-SPIRED WRITINGS

****

ABOUT THE DRAWINGS AND GRAPHICS

The drawings and paintings in this book were first done as an enjoyment and an attempt to get back into doing drawings and painting. I had not drawn nor painted for many, many years. These drawings have not been perfected because at the time I had not intended to use them publicly, and never did I think I would be putting them into a book! I decided to leave them the way they are. Since this book is one of inspired and immediate intuitional work, it seemed right and fitting for these to not only be used in this book, but also, to leave them the way they first came forth.

I had done the drawing/painting with the caption: "Calling the Sacred" approximately in the year 1993; and the one: "Closer to that which we are" in the year 1999 or there about; and the drawing called: "and the mist parted giving way to the light" was done in 1997. "Weaving the Memories, Weaving the Dream" was finished in approximately the year 2007. I had started it around 1990 and later decided to add it to the book, and so began finishing it in the year 2007. The other three drawings were first scribbles. The one I entitled: "In search of the lost child" began the scribble drawings… it began in approx. the year 2006 with the scribble of a three-year-old girl. The drawing: "In search of the lost child" began from that child of three's aqua blue crayon scribbling. I had gone to visit my daughter Shelly and her children. They were out by the pool of the apartment building they called home. A mother, with her three-year-old daughter, had been watching me, as were a few others who later also approached me. The mother with the little girl came over to me with a smile and asked to speak to me. She then said she sensed a high spiritual energy about me and asked me if I would do a blessing of her apartment for things there were very heavy and negative, affecting her family. I had gone to her basement apt. and before we began the child asked me if I would draw and color with her. I said yes, and she told me to set down on the couch. She handed me the aqua blue crayon scribble and went to her room to get more crayons and paper. While she was gone, I looked at her aqua blue crayon scribbling. After a while I began to sense and see a figure within the randomly done child scribble. The little girl told me I could keep her scribble. At home I again studied the scribbling and then I took a ballpoint pen and began tracing over only the aqua blue lines that my eyes saw making an image. I left the rest of the blue scribble as it was. What you see when you look at chapter two's drawing: "In search of the lost child", is the original scribble and the original paper she had done the scribbled on. If you look closely, you will discover what I did not notice until much later: The top and bottom of the paper she scribbled on has geographic designs, which are all sacred. Coincidence? Is there such a thing? To this scribble I added stars, and with the ballpoint pen I created zig-zags on the blue crayon scribbles she had extended above the figure I saw in her scribble. I then added stars above them. I did this due to what I was feeling this image stood for. After that I became interested in seeing if I could do this with mine and other's scribbles. I began with my four granddaughters. I had each of them use one, or as many colors as they wished, and had them scribble randomly all over the paper. What I discovered was fascinating! I could concentrate on the scribbles and see images there! I next traced these images in the format I saw, and it then made them visible for others to see as well. I saw people, animals, dimensional beings, the scribbler's fears, their joys, and their spiritual helpers. I looked at all this and I began to discern what the person who had made the scribble was going through and other things concerning that person, just as I'd been able to discerned about the child and what was going on in her home and with her. It was as though the scribbles held within them a energy, a message of deeper meaning about the one who put forth that energy into the scribble. It was like a blue print…an imprinting of energy put on paper and revealed to me. I decided to do my own scribbling and see what came forth to me. The results of two of these scribbles I have included in this book. They are: "Stirring the Stars" and "The Keys to the Heavens". These two drawings were created in the same way as I did the other scribbles: tracing only what was being revealed to me as I traced over some of the scribble that I had made, randomly and quickly, with no directing of the paint nor color medium used. I was however, centered in my spirit in quantum spiritual intention. I also was thinking of wanting to see a spiritual figure. One began to appear. I had not a thought of what it would be nor look like. I wanted it to happen without my intentional directing. The drawings came forth to me as new and unexpected, revealed images for me to contemplate on and feel and learn of the message they held. They are therefore not symmetrical in a form considered perfect by some people's standards. On further study of what has come forth from these drawings, I've come to believe that they are divinely and "other world" given, for not just myself but for others, therefore, for to be included in The Books of "IS".

As I'd looked upon the drawings I felt intuitively led to add symbols, numbers, sacred geometry, spirals, lines and various other markings representing life's mysteries and what the majority of humans cannot yet understand with the "blinders" they presently wear over their senses and all knowing "eye". The other four drawings I had done over a span of years, also fitted in with the book, and with that in mind I began looking at them in a different light. I then allowed spirit to direct me, and so I added symbols to *them* as well. These seven drawings, one for each chapter's beginning, are for your meditation and spirit. Perhaps they will invoke Divine memories, stirring your "stars", your DNA memories, to the truth of life and who and what you are and how very special and important you are to the totality of the universe.

The quotes I have included that are from others, and noted in back of this book under notations, were added *AFTER* I'd completed the writings within this book. They, like the drawings and star designs, made their way to me unexpected, unconsciously and unintentionally by me. I came across the quotes that are from others, with no searching, nor intention of using any quotes made by others. I had not planned on using anyone else's quotes in my book, but these quotes seemed to validate to me what I was saying in this book. They fitted in with my book's purpose so well that I decided to add them to this book, giving those who had said those quotes credibility.

The star designs and word images first came forth after I had decided to add stars due to mainly two reasons: First, I'd noticed that some of my sentences and paragraphs had ended with only a few words extending to the next line. In some of the writings this appeared unbalanced to me, and so I decided to center the short lines and leave the long ones. After I'd completed the first page I had done this to, I noticed that by doing this, there was created an image that, if there were eyes added to it, would appear as a image of a mobile animal or being. I decided to go ahead and add the stars for eyes, and to me the image stood out even more! Since the book is about spirit, and involves the cosmos and Heavenly Hosts, stars for eyes, and as additions for contemplations, seemed fitting; and so lead to my creating the hearts, the mandala star alignment, and the other star formations; many being created (so-called, "accidental") as if by an invisible hand other then my physical one. For example: I had decided to add stars at the end of the story about Solo. It seem the thing to do because it seemed to go along with the story: of creation, the galaxy and the universe, therefore: stars! I'd randomly added stars, and at different sizes, *also* randomly. Then suddenly the stars were all highlighted and brought to the center. I had not hit the highlight key, nor, the centering button. I was at first moment, displeased that this happened for I had thought it had deleted or really messed up the work I had just completed. But that was only for a second. The next second I seen what was created from that strange occurrence! There, before me, appeared to be a star creature! Come together into a form made from random stars of various sizes on a page! This began me to thinking this was no accident; therefore neither were all the other images coming forth without my directly nor intentionally doing. I knew I therefore needed to keep them this way. Yet, doing this presented extra delay, work, and challenges for the publisher (Author House) and me: I turned to my friend Daniel Bingamon to help me to adjust my computer to higher resolutions and put it on adobe to "freeze" it for the Publisher to see what could be done to keep it that way. This meant that this book could then be reduced to where some of the writings would be difficult to read, and I would also have to give up having them in hard back. If I let the margarines be adjusted to the publisher's usual manner, it would shift the designs, destroying them! It is my hope that the reader will be able to benefit from these images and drawings as they came forth to me for you, and that the words printed in this book can be comfortably and possible for you to read.

On the star drawings of the hearts, I was unable to get the left side to move forward nor back so they appear not so rounded. Is that also something to ponder upon?

The entire Book of "IS" is one of serendipity created by powers beyond just *my* doings. This book is written and created with Divine intervention for *all* of us! It is written in a way to assist in the expansion of the mind and conscience, and to activate your higher self, your holy spirit, (known by many as: the Shekinah) thereby connecting and accessing your divinity. And it is for those who are *ready*! It is therefore written in a metaphorical and poetic form. Many call this: parables. This is the language of light. It is the language of Love… It is the Music of the Spheres…the Angels "singing"…this rhythmic metaphorical (parables: com- parables) and story manner of "hearing" (the "ear" to hear) and "seeing" (the "eye" to see). It allows you your free will to "see and hear" what you are ready to see and hear and understand and know. Truth will open the enter "eye" when you are *ready* to see. The enter "ear's" "door way" to the hearing of the knowing will call to you, and you will hear the Golden Knodd… the singing of the Spheres.

The drawings and the word and star graphics are meditations. View them quietly and peacefully. Study them. Meditate upon them. They are tools for your spiritual awakening and advancement. This entire Book of "IS", and the future Books and CDs are tools for your spirit, your soul, and mind…a gift of love from the greatest love beyond the beyond….

Blessings, Dear Ones

Lovingly,
Dr. R. Lowery-Hawk
The Author

BIO OF THE AUTHOR

Dr. R. Lowery-Hawk is a descendent of Native American Indian and European Ancestry. Her Native American blood-line is mostly tsa la gi (Cherokee). She recalls receiving, at the young age of five, teaching from "*somewhere*" in the form of "knowings". They came to her seeming as *her* thoughts through wondering, observing, and questioning, which let her to "experimenting". As she did so, knowledge and wisdom came forth in her mind, which felt to her to be truth. She would also receive visions: images in her mind, of a long ago time on Earth. She would receive all these things, mostly, when she was alone, and mostly, out in nature, sitting on the Earth, playing "in" the earth, (making mud pies, and the likes); or while she observed the life on the ground and all around her. She would then test some of the teachings she was receiving. Other "knowings" were simply that: *knowing*, Natural, instinctive, knowing. Her young child mind did not question these Knowings, and they always proved to be true. They came naturally to her, feeling natural, and so they were not strange to her young mind. She never questioned them.

Many painful and lonely events in Ruby's life pushed her deeper within herself and into solitude, nature, and her inquisitive mind. She then, through observation of others, learned how too much of hurting, and feeling other's anger and violence with out understanding and empathy can affect even those with the best of intensions of love. She found it could draw out of one, the aggressive and defensive actions of preservation, sometimes in the form of: anger and violence; the very things one disliked and did not want to be nor be around. As she thought about all this, it seemed to her that the people, of all ages, she had met so far, were detached from life: life around them, others, their self and the love they were capable of and wanted. It seemed they were detached from love and a divine reality and purpose. They were detached from their *true* self and Divine heritage. People she had encountered at that time, seemed so angry, unhappy, selfish and cruel. As a young child she would think: "Everyone seems so mean, (that she'd experience so far at that time) I don't fit in with them. Where is my home, friends, and family? I miss them and the kindness and love. I want to go back home." She spent her entire childhood alienated from others, by others, and the beauty of joy, love and belonging that would have went with it. She felt alienated from feeling *truly* understood and loved by others. During that time, she turned more and more to nature, finding her peace and love *there*, observing and feeling the beauty and love around her and within her, calling to her and teaching her. The ant became her first "doctoring"; her first "patient" and "experimenting", that the "something" was guiding her to, so to teach her the first lesson on the life energy in *all* things. The "something" began by telling her of the life force inside the ant, and told her: *that* was the ant. The "something" told her *why* the ant, and other insects *seemed* to leave their bodies quicker then most other species, and *what* the ant needed to bring it back into an undamaged body. The reason they left so quickly was because of what today she knows is referred to as: shock or fear and acceptance. This “Something” was teaching her about insects, and how to help in the restoration of the life essences in all things. She did not know, at that young age, the words: life force, essence or the other terminologies. She only “knew” what she sensed and was given as a knowing through curiosity, brought on by loneliness, sadness and a desire for understanding and pleasure in living. These experiences were like a knowing of truth...that was the way the “teachings” felt: like a curiosity moving to a deeper wisdom and sensing of actuality-truth, with no doubting: Natural, innate. The “teachings” then were to also teach her about herself, other life, its spirit, its life essence and how we use it to bring about birth or “death”. To “doctor” the ant “patient”, she used a stiff blade of grass to stimulate it, gently, back into “remembering” it was only “sleeping” and its body undamaged and capable of sustaining its life energy. Ruby was six years old. She knew by the age of seven, she wanted to be a “healer”, a “make-things-well-and-better” person. She was taught about stones from this “something” and about many other things including: plants, trees, bees, birds, the wind, rain, snow, and, thunder and lightning.

She could feel “things” (such as Earth Devas/Spirits) “unseen”, observing her, curious, as she walked observing life around her in the woods. She was not frightened but intrigued. The woods and outdoor life became her family and friends; the earth then, was her playmate and (one of) her teacher…her comforter, her guide, family, and her enjoyment. In nature she felt loved and at peace. All this was the beginning of her journey within. It was the “stepping stones” that lead her to her self-realization, and understanding of her empathic and spiritual gifts. Her experiences with people, nature and her aloneness with her own feelings and observations taught her that love and beauty were indeed all around and within her, *everyone,* and *ALL things*, and that realizing this brought it *inside of you*. Many years later, she began to come to the conclusion that the reason so many people felt so lonely, lost and angry was because they had become detached from nature, their true self, and detached from their higher self and a higher power that created them and this planet. They were “locked” in a “dark place” of sorrow, fear, guilt, and, feelings of over whelming hopelessness. They were like lost souls who saw no way out, for they had lost sight of the truth of life and the truth of who they truly are, and they had not gained trust. They could not find answers to their seeking of love, happiness, the meaning of life, the purpose of their existence, and the truth of *all* things. They had lost the “knowing”, the Divine language of light, and the memory connection to what the yearning inside them was, and what they were destined to be. Ruby did not, however, come to that conclusion until she was an adult. As a child and young woman, she simply realized people seemed lost and desperate for all the things that should have been natural for them and for them to have, if only they would open their heart to love and trust, giving compassion and all the gifts of love, without all the negative emotions and thoughts attached to them. She began to feel anger also moving in her and so she made a decision, while she was still a child, that she would *choose* the path of kindness and empathy, over a choice of acting out and becoming one of revenge, hate, and violence. And so, began her many "tests" and "trials" on balancing organic life, and the Spirit, on its way of uniting with God-Goddess Soul by uniting *again* with the "Over-Soul" (Higher Self-Super Un-conscience), Angelic Hosts, the Great and Holy Spirit (Shekinah) and the Earth Mother.

Now in the present time, Dr. R. Lowery-Hawk is an elder and mother of three children, and a Grandmother of five. She has one son and three daughters, and four granddaughters and one grandson: (Her son's son passed to the other side at the age of three years and eight months.) She loves and enjoys her children and grandchildren very much! She enjoys the outdoors, camping, animals, plants, libraries; and among many other things, learning about natural and alternative medicines and health. She loves learning about herbs and natural foods, straight from the yard and fields. Dr. Ruby Lowery-Hawk enjoys learning many things about life, including primitive skills and deeper truths of creation and creator. She enjoys, very much, being with her Native American "Family"; dancing at the celebrations; drumming, singing, and socializing with her friends and family while spending time in nature, camping, and sitting around the fire while they enjoy singing, drumming and sharing laughter, stories, poems and wholesome food and warm drinks. She enjoys and loves the learning and researching she does; writing; drawing; painting; sculpturing; creating; and all that she does and has learned so far. She looks forward to learning more skills; learning more about life; the Great Mystery; and her Ancestors. She looks forward to bringing forth more spiritual gifts, gifts that *all people* have innately available and are meant to access to use for their betterment, and for the healing and betterment of the *entire Human race,* not forgetting our Dear Earth Mother and *all* the life here and beyond here!

Dr. R. Lowery-Hawk is a channel for Galactic messages and other truths of a high spiritual nature, meant to assist others and self in a good way. She is also a spiritual teacher; licensed, anointed, and ordained minister; a Doctor of Divinity; a Doctor of Religious Science; A Philosopher of Religion; A Mystic; Metaphysician; Intuitive Energy Worker-assisting in healing; a "Medium"; Philosopher; Poet; Story-Teller; Artist; Teacher; Writer; Actress; and Facilitator of several modalities of self-empowerment and wellness techniques. She is the former producer and host of a television show entitled: "Equipoise: in quest of balance". She also works with and teaches: meditation and visualization; trance and ceremonial-movement-dance; ancient spiritual knowledge; mysticism and wisdom; spirit/automatic and channeled writing and drawing; herbs; plants;

nature; and natural foods for one's health and well being. She has an strong interest in learning and discovery so she researches the above things listed, along with her interest in truth; wisdom; spiritual and ancient knowledge; mysticism; life; multi-cultures and their people; in a quantum level/depth, and entirety. Some of her interests include: string theory; physics; science; the body's chakras; dowsing, meditation; visualization; chanting; mandalas; affirmations; song; dance; prayer; power of the mind, emotions, and words; higher consciousness; ancient truths and ancient religions; (including today's many spiritual belief systems) and life experiences. She also researches natural health and well-being methods and results, plus information on modern medicines and treatments. Dr. Lowery-Hawk has been initiated in the Priest/Priestess "Brotherhood" of the "Feather Plumed Serpent"---a Native American Mystery School. (The Feather Plumed Serpent stands for the energy of the Great Spirit/Great Mystery: God/Christ energy; and for life here, on and within the Earth: water, and the spiraling movement life moves in: circles within circles/spiraling. It also stands for wisdom of life and it's "secrets, its "mysteries", plus so much more in depth.) Dr. R. Lowery-Hawk has also been initiated in several other Ancient Mystery Schools, including Christian Mysteries, for over 35 years. She is also a wellness/health intuitive. She has, for over thirty-years, researched and learned holistic and intuitive means of putting, and maintaining, the *whole* person (body, mind, spirit, and emotions) back into balance. * (She used this learning and spiritual attunement with the Creator and ancestors, the planet earth, the stars, and her DNA, to save her own life when her body was so badly stricken with illness.) She is also trained spiritually, intuitively and instinctively, tapping into "the knowing", in other modalities of healing of the whole person. Being a licensed minister, she incorporates the laying on of hands along with spiritual counseling/guidance and teachings. Many refer to what she does as: an energy healing and a wellness worker, with intuitive attuning and channeling. Healing Touch and axial tonal attunement are two of the energy workings she does for others and self. When Dr. Lowery-Hawk works with a client, she attunes with the person, or subject's energy field and the Universal Energies, Creator-God/Goddess, the Star Nations, Ancestral Healing Spirits, and Mother Earth, intuitively accessing information, sensing where to direct Creator's energy (with or without the laying on of hands or visual-emotional and sound directing). This is to help assist in the person's journey; well being, and body balancing for the healing of spirit; thus, moving to all aspects of the whole person, including one's body and attuning to one's self-defeating habitual thinking. While doing this, she channels a matrix of energy and information from the Creator and Divine Spirit; Creator's Spirit helpers; Holy Galactic helpers; Akashic Records; and the Divine DNA memories; sensing and working on a cellular level, receiving, many times, "messages" for the client/subject..

* **POST NOTE**: **1**. Dr. R. Lowery-Hawk was using a lot of energy and time doing a lot of empathic and physical work for others and not enough for herself, and so, in 1996 her body started shutting down. For over thirteen years, and, most times, five days a week, she saw health specialists for documentation. She realized she was "dying". She put all her trust in the higher powers of Creator, the loving and all powerfully complete God; God's assistants from most high; and the higher powers of the Earth. She also "listened" to her body, utilizing Spirit attunement with it and all that would and could assist her in her recovery. Some of the modalities she applied were: faith, prayer; dreams; visions; synchronicity awareness; dreams; the healing ancestors; and the encoded healing memories within her cells and DNA. She knew she had to trust in these higher powers. She had to trust her intuitive guidance from these powers that she believes comes from a power source many refer to as love energy: God/Goddess, so that her body and all aspects of her, as a whole person, could balance and heal. She then needed to recall and utilize what she had experienced, learned, was taught from life, others, and the Spirit world. She had to practice fully, now, on herself what she had taught others in the pass. She also knew, she had to allow: **Love**. She needed to give herself more love. She needed to believe, *truly believe,* in the power of love and goodness; the love of others; *and* the love *within* herself. (See *2) She therefore, relied upon the Creator and his/her higher powers and the "synchronicity of things" in her life to put her---*bring her,* into that sacred place that resides within. She needed to stay connected to the "knowings", so to connect her with whom and whatever was needed for her health - for her life! The results were: she lived! Her health has been greatly re-stored; and, "she" was able to continue writing this book so you can experience, or, further experience, having validation of truths you, yourself may have been receiving, that are referred to by many as: visions and miracles!

2. In 1996 the Author became chronically and seriously ill. She had pushed herself too hard, trying to do too much to help others and her family. Helping friends, family, and others spiritually, and sometimes, financially required she work longer hours and more jobs, leaving only a couple hours of sleep. She worked seven days and nights, giving up most of her sleep, money and many times, food, to do this. Then, less then half a year after receiving the intuitive spirit message that she would become ill and "touch life and 'death's' door", (pass from her physical body to not return to it) Dr. Lowery-Hawk did in fact become deathly ill. Her body began shutting down. The telepathic message from the Spirit world told her she would have to apply what the "Healing Angels" and "Ancestors" had been teaching her if she was to stay in her body and on Earth. She was given "permission" and choice, to leave this plane or, to stay. If she stayed and did as they directed her, and had been teaching her for many years, she would learn and earn, more healing gifts to help others and self. They told her she had to think of her self also and apply the things she does for, and teaches others, to herself as well, even if it meant taking time away from others. They told her, "One must love their self and care for that self or they will have committed a 'sin' against their self and the Holy Spirit. "If she choose to stay—"live", and applied their teaching to herself, resting and slowing down, she would learn more on healing so to help others. They told her, her illness was ***also*** because she was being offered a choice: to stay or cross over, for reasons she understood. They also told her that the illness was to provide her with more teachings and lessons, by becoming the illnesses so to know it intimately, and the illnesses came to give her a message to slow down and take time for her self. This time of healing would later ***"STILL"*** her so she could return back to the book they were co-writing with her. Plus, "stilling" her so she could finish walking her path on Earth. They, the messengers, from the place of knowing, said they were waiting for her readiness to continue. The Author said: "They were very loving and patient". They would accept whatever she chose concerning all this. They had said (in a "knowing" feeling) that they were patient and waited for her to make the choice whether to do the book or not to. The choice was still hers, and when she was ready, they were there and would guide her and assist her. She chose to stay! She had at that time, two "living" grand children: Fantashia, three years of age, and Dartanyon, one year. She wanted to be with them as they grew, helping guide them and teaching them here on earth, loving them, enjoying them, plus experiencing them, ***with them,*** in every moment of their growing. She loved them greatly and loved being with them. She also wanted to do whatever she could to help Mother Earth and to help others. She truly wanted to complete this book and the series, plus the others she has been writing and planning on writing to publish. She wanted to continue teaching and counseling, and she wanted to learn more about the "Mysteries" of creation and life. She was learning as she connected with the Holy Spirit, receiving the writings; and she enjoyed the ecstasy of that beautiful connection. She wanted to write more and receive more from those beautiful caring "Above Beings"! She wanted to learn more! Assist more! Some of the writings/messages came from her higher self (Over-Soul, Super Con- science), others from other "Nations" of higher planes. ***All*** were caring messengers, doing loving work, aiding the good of Human kind, this planet, and all the other planets and galaxies we, and this planet, affect. Ruby then asked the Creator and the Creator's Healing Spirits to heal her as she slept, for she was too weak to stay awake and assist. She would assist in the other realm. She asked to stay if that was in the best interest for the good of Earth and her Soul's purpose in being here. She said to them, *if* she were meant to leave this Earth plane, then she would prepare herself for that journey. She asked that she be lead to *whoever* and *whatever* could help her. She trusted and began to receive "messages" on what to do. She experienced synchronicity: being at the right places at the right time, where she'd receive information or she'd attune to words, symbols, impressions, or thought pictures: visions, which she felt innately were true. These synchronicities lead her, guided her, to what she should do and what she should put in her body to assist her in its healing. She also applied her intuition for herself so she would know what her body and spirit were telling her about her illnesses, and what (she) was needing to put her whole person back into balance. She was dying... But, the loving Spirit world assisted her in the surviving of the illnesses and bypassing the transition of spirit from her body. It would take fifteen more years before she would have the writings put into typed book-ready format. Fifteen more years of patience with her weakened health that challenged her every day in such away she had neither the strength, time, money, nor availability to edit, type and prepare the writings for publishing. She lived, and lives, in a rural area, and had given her car away due to her illness and her inability to work so to afford a car; plus her daughter needed a car, since someone had totaled hers. For seven years, without transportation, she relied upon Divine enter venison to get her places and help her to survive. She had also asked the Creator, The "Old Ones" (The Galactic Star Beings), and Creator's high hierarchy, to help her to complete and publish this book if it were *truly* something that should be made public, and would help others. Each time she asked for help, they helped. But challenges kept presenting themselves. It seemed the writings were to wait until the right time: the selected, chosen year to be published. Now that chosen time has arrived! A twenty-seven year span of writings is now ready! These books are for you! They are a gift not just from Dr. R. Lowery-Hawk, but also from those on the most high. They are for you Dear Reader and they are a love offering for the Human race! It was not an accident you came across them. They found you!

Enjoy, and welcome to your journey within:

THE BOOKS OF "IS"!

*** Dr. R. Lowery-Hawk has written several books**
(Some still in process).
She plans on having at least seven in total, of the series of:
The Books of "IS"
*** Some of the books she's written,**
And plans to make available for the public are:

* "How the Grizzly Bear got his hair and medicine"
Plus three other books on the little people)
* "The Space Between the Worlds"
(A Spiritual Sci-fi Fantasy Novel series)
* "Camellia, child of despair"
(An story for awareness on child and parent depression/abuse)
* "Tempest of the forest: The lost child"
* "The Tiger walks when the Eagle Cries"
(A poetry book of stories)
* "The Spirit of Real Food": Eating LIGHT
(A food and recipes cook book for ascension)

****THE BOOKS OF "IS" : BOOK ONE***
is the Author's, and the Hierarchy's first choice to be published.

****The Author is single, residing in rural Ohio, with her "fur-family" of dogs and cats.***

**** Requests for information and speaking engagements****
Contact Website:
*

www.littlemiamiartisans.com/drrlowery

E-mail: equipoise.inquestof@yahoo.com

To order more books, go to: www.authorhouse.com or Author's above website.

Keep your thoughts gentle and loving. Imagine and feel all the beauty this world can be, and it shall be! Be joyful! All good is observing you, to give to you the same.

GLOSSARY

AKASHA/AKASHIC RECORDS: It has been said that *Kasha is a Sanskrit word, meaning: "Primary substance", which all things are formed from. It is said to be the first stage of the crystallization of Spirit. All primordial substance is Spirit. Matter is Spirit moving at a lower rate of vibration, becoming a coagulum. The primary substance (Akasha), is very exquisitely fine, and is so sensitive that the slightest vibrations of ether any place in the Universe register an indelible impression upon it. It is everywhere present. It is the "Universal Mind".

When the mind of man is in exact accord with the Universal Mind, man enters recognition consciously of these Akasha impressions, and may collect them and translate them into any language of Earth in which he is familiar. These imperishable records of life, known as the Akashic Records, are in the domain of Supreme Intelligence, or Universal Mind, and the reader of them must be in such a close touch with the Holy Spirit/Holy Breath/Supreme Intelligence that every thought vibration is instantly felt in every fiber of his being. Knowledge of any kind can be obtained from the Universal Mind, which is Supreme Intelligence, called by Oriental scholars: The Akasha Records, and by the Hebrew masters: ***The Book of God's Remembrance.***

ALCHEMY: Webster's dictionary: 1.The medieval chemical science and speculative philosophy, whose aims were the transmutation of the base metal gold; the discovery of a universal cure for disease and the discovery of a means of indefinitely prolonging life. 2. A great magic power of transformation. The New International Webster's Pocket Dictionary 2002: An ancient art dedicated to unlocking the mysteries of universal healing, eternal youth, and the changing of base metals into gold.

ARCHCHETYPE: Webster's Dictionary: 1.The original model, form, or pattern from which something is made or from which something develops. 2. In Platonism: One of the ideas of which existent things are imitations-compare idea b. In scholastic philosophy: the idea in the divine intellect that determines the form of created thing. c. In Loche: one of the external realities with which our ideas and impressions to some extent corresponds .3a. A primitive generalized plan of structure deduced from the characters of the members of a natural group of animals or plants and assumed to be the type from which they have been modified. b. The original ancestors of a group or animals or plants. 4. In the psychology of C.G. Jung: an inherited idea or mode of thought derived from the experience of the race and present in the unconscious of the individual.

ALCHEMY: From Webster's dictionary 1.The medieval chemical science and speculative philosophy, whose aims were the transmutation of the base metal gold; the discovery of a universal cure for disease and the discovery of a means of indefinitely prolonging life. 2. A great magic power of transformation. The New International Webster's Pocket Dictionary 2002: An ancient art dedicated to unlocking the mysteries of universal healing, eternal youth, and the changing of base metals into gold.

ARCHCHETYPE: Webster's Dictionary: 1. The original model, form, or pattern from which something is made or from which something develops. 2. In Platonism: One of the ideas of which existent things are imitations-compare idea b. in scholastic philosophy: the idea in the divine intellect that determines the form of created thing. c. In Loche: one of the external realities with which our ideas and impressions to some extent corresponds .3a. A primitive generalized plan of structure deduced from the characters of the members of a natural group of animals or plants and assumed to be the type from which they have been modified. b. the original ancestors of a group or animals or plants. 4a. In the psychology of C.G. Jung: an inherited idea or mode of thought derived from the experience of the race and present in the unconscious of the individual; characters of the members of a natural group of animals or plants and assumed to be the type from which they have been modified. 4b. The original ancestors of a group or animals or plants.

5.In the psychology of C.G. Jung: an inherited idea or mode of thought derived from the experience of the race and present in the unconscious of the individual.

ECSTASY: From Webster's Dictionary: To fill with ecstasy or rapture. Enraptured (the most ecstasied order holy who is subject to states of enrapture: enrapture)...Ecstoric- a person who is subject to states resembling trance. The International Pocket Dictionary 2002: emotional rapture or delight.

METAPHOR: Webster's dictionary: 1. A figure of speech in which a word or phrase denoting one kind of object or action is used in place of another to suggest a likeness or analogy between them (as in the ship plows the seas or in a volley of oaths): an implied comparison (as in a marble brow) in contrast to the explicit comparison of the smile (as in a brow white as marble)-compare. Trope.

METAPHYSICS: From Webster's dictionary 1. A particular system or theory of (view of nature and man's place in nature.) 2. The system of first principles of philosophy underlying a particular study or subject of inquiry; relating to external nature, a division of philosophy that includes ontology and cosmology—relationships obtained between the underlying reality and its manifestations. The New International Webster's Pocket Dictionary 2002: The branch of philosophy that deals with the essential nature of reality.

MYSTIC: Webster's Dictionary, 1987: A subject to mystical experiences. A follower or an expounder of a mystical way of life; a person iniative of mystery.

MYSTICISM: From Webster's third new international dictionary, 1987: 1. Belief in direct or intuitive attainment of communion of God or spiritual truths. 2. Any doctrine that knowledge of spiritual truths may be obtained intuitively. Webster's dictionary, 1993: 1.The experience of mystical union or direct communion with ultimate reality reported by mystics. 2. A theory of mystical knowledge: The doctrine or belief that direct knowledge of God, of spiritual truth, ultimate reality, or insight, or illumination and in a way differing from ordinary sense perception or rationation (nature) 3.Anything postulating or based on the possibility of direct and intuitive acquisition of ineffable knowledge or power. The New International Webster's Pocket Dictionary, 2002: 1. A belief in a reality beyond the understanding or comprehension of the senses.

MYTH: Webster's dictionary, 1971 & 1987: 1. A traditional story serving to explain some phenomenon: Mythology is the richest source of symbols. It is the language of religion. All ancient religions were mystery religions and manifested through symbols. All sacred books, including the bible are written in symbolic language. The universe consisted of matter of various shapes and sizes, moving in space and time.

PHILOSOPHER: From Webster's dictionary: 1. One who seeks wisdom or enlightenment: reflective thinker. Scholar, investigator, traditionally is thought of as a person whose chief interest is an attempt to discover the innermost essence of reality. 2. A specialist in the synthesis of knowledge.

PHILOSOPHIC: Webster's dictionary: 1. Of or relating to philosopher or philosophy (the very dogma that God is everywhere—a considerable knowledge of. 2. Imbued with or characterized by the attitude of a philosopher (that breath of outlook which distinguishes the mind---long term attitude towards life.

PHILOSOPHY: The New International Webster's Pocket Dictionary 2002: 1. The study of knowledge; a fundamental principle; a system of beliefs.

SHA-MAN:* The book: The world of Shamansism (New views of an ancient tradition): By Roger Walsh, M.D, PhD. Published by Llewellyn Publications. A shaman is a traveler and explorer in a world most other people do not see. The word shaman comes from the word saman, from the language of Tungus people in Siberia. It means: one who is excited, moved, or raised. They are often said to be in an "ecstatic state" when they work. Ecstasy means "moved out of one's self"---a state of intense joy and awe. The shaman's soul flies freely anywhere, though time and space to distant places on Earth or to other worlds. They do this by going into a different state of awareness. Some experts have traced shamanism all the way back to the beginning of religion on earth. Archeological evidence suggests that shamanic methods are at least 20 nor 30,000 yrs. Old---shamans are medicine people---healers. The shaman must communicate with the spirit world to diagnose problems and bring back the soul. All shamans are healers, but not all medicine people are shamans. The shaman is a figure of great power and wisdom. Shamanism is our common human condition and our common past---Michael Harner (Wrote the way of the Shaman), says most shamans are chosen or called by the spirits.

SEEKER: One who is conscious ("awakening" or has "awakened"), to the realization that s/he and life has more purpose, and then begins seeking the higher truths of Creator, life, self, and all other "mysteries" pertaining to the universe of all that exist. They seek truth and what and who they and "God" are.

SHA-MANISM: From the book: The world of Shamanism by Roger Walsh, M.D, PhD. (New views of an Ancient tradition) Publisher: Llewellyn Publications. A Voluntary and variations of practices focusing on entering altered states of conscience whey one experiences themselves or their spirit(s) interacting with other spirits or enities in other realms. 2. A technique of ecstasy. 3. A Tungus verb for shaman is saman: "To refer to persons of both sexes who at their will, voluntary induce spirits into themselves know". And it and use their power over the spirits for their own interest and to help others who suffer from spirits. A Shaman controls his/her states of conscience-altered states of conscience (A.S.C.'s). They enter into a controlled ASC on behalf of their community. 4. Out of body experiences/soul flight; a conscious discipline; a spiritual and a healing discipline.

SHEKINAH: Definition from the Keys Of Enoch written down by J.J. Hurtak: 1. (Heb. 'Divine presence / Name of Holy Spirit) 2. The "presence of God"; the sanctification of the molecular form of the inner universe by the Holy Spirit. Christian Bible: 1. The "Dove"; Peace. 2. Holy Ghost; 3.Spirit/Feminine aspect of God

SHEKINAH UNIVERSE: Keys of Enoch – J.J .Hurtak : The inner universe created for the transformation of the basic building blocks of intelligence out of the sea of the Eternal to go into the presence of the father (God)..

SIN: Keys of Enoch – J.J. Hutak: 1. The consciousness of limitation as result of the Failure of spiritual-biological experiments. "Sin"-1. Anything that prevents the "living Light" of the Infinite Mind from being 'creatively recycled' through the body vehicle. 2. The consciousness of having a talent and not using it for the benefit of mankind.

SPIRAL: Webster's Dictionary

THE GREAT MYSTERY: 1. All that is, the power that creates all that is, and what it is and why; 2. The unknown; 3. God/Goddess; 4. The void.

UNIVERSE: 1. Uni (one); Verse (song); 2. The one and the many (united); 3. All of creation; and beyond our awareness.

WISDOM: Webster's Third New Dictionary, 1993: 1. the effectual mediating principle or personification of God's will in the creation of the world: Logos. 2a. accumulated information: philosophic or scientific learning: knowledge (all the---of the agės...available at negligible cost to all of us within the covers of books---Bennett Cerf) 3a archaic: an embodiment of wisdom: aphorism. 4. the teachings of the ancient wise men relating to the art of living and sometimes to philosophical problems concerning the universe, man, or God and forming a class of literature represented in the Hebrew book of Job, Proverbs, Ecclesiastes, Ecclesiasticus, and the wisdom of Solomon. Syn. 1. Wisdom: from spiritual literature: The feminine; the Shekinah; the Holy Ghost, which is one of the aspects of God. **God:** the creating force of all the universe.

Sha-man: I have spelled Shaman with a hyphen because some people pronounce it as shame-mon or shame man; plus, It was also brought to my attention that some, therefore, believe it means : One in shame; being shamed or deserving shame. This of course, is far, far from the truth, as you can read from its definition plus any research you may do.

ANNOTATIONS

1.* Ancient Vedic Saying, from the small book entitled: "Moving Forward, Keeping Still, The Gateway to Eastern Wisdom (A Book Of Quotations), Ariel Books, by, Andrews and McMeel, Kansas City. Copyright: 1997 by Armand Eisen.

2.* Big Thunder, quote out of the miniature book: Native American Wisdom, put out by Running Press, 1993.

3.* Black Elk, quote from the miniature book: Native American Wisdom, Put out By: Running Press, 1993.

4.* Chased by Bears, quote out of the miniature book: Native American Wisdom, put out by Running Press, 1993.

5.* Geshe Kelsang Gyaatso, from the small book entitled: "Moving Forward, Keeping Still, The Gateway to Eastern Wisdom (A Book Of Quotations), Ariel Books, by Andrews and McMeel, Kansas City. Copyright: 1997 by Armand Eisen.

6.* Jesus: from the King James version of the Christian Bible.

7.* Luther Standing Bear, quote out of the miniature book: Native American Wisdom, put out by: Running Press, 1993

8.* J.J. Hutak, from his book: The Keys of Enoch. See # 14.

9.* Marcus Antonius, quote from book entitled: "Moving Forward, Keeping Still, The Gateway to Eastern Wisdom (A Book Of Quotations), Ariel Books, by, Andrews and McMeel, Kansas City. Copright: 1997 by Armand Eisen.

10.* Michael Harner, From his books on Shamanism.

11* Morning Dove (Christine Quinasket), quote from the miniature book entitled: Native American Wisdom, by Running Press,1993

12.* Muniel Rukeyser, quote from the small book entitled: "Moving Forward, Keeping Still, The Gateway to Eastern Wisdom (A Book Of Quotations),Ariel Books, by, Andrews and McMeel, Kansas City. Copyright: 1997 by Armand Eisen.

13.* Plato, quote from the small book entitled: "Moving Forward, Keeping Still, The Gateway to Eastern Wisdom (A Book Of Quotations), Ariel Books, by, Andrews and McMeel, Kansas City. Copright: 1997 by Armand Eisen.

14.* Some definitions from The glossary are from: The Book of knowledge: The keys of Enoch by J.J. Hurtak: third edition 1987,1992. Published by: The Academy for future science.

ACKNOWLEDGEMENTS

I'd like to thank first and foremost, The Great Mystery-Creator, who goes by many names, be it God or Goddess, Great Spirit, Holy Ghost, Over-soul, Shekinah, Yahweh, Jehovah, Supreme Intelligence, Father, Mother; Grandfather, Grandmother; or any of the various names given over the thousands of years to that Great Mystery force that creates all that we now know of and all we do not yet remember. I acknowledge these Superior powers seen and unseen by the human eye, and all the unseen forces from this loving creator source that have been assisting me and are instrumental in my receiving guidance in these writings, and their manifestation into book form. This includes: The Angelic hosts, (The Celestial Hierarchy); The Ancient Ones: The Star Nations/Relations; The Old Ones; Mother Earth and all her earthen self/children, my Ancestors; my Spiritual Masters and Guides; and the Shekinah: "The Dove"; My Over-Soul (Higher Self); The Holy Spirit; Galactic Federation; All Spiritual Messengers; and the many Guides of the many dimensions/worlds of Love, Light and sound, and all other helpers of love and light. The Great Mystery Creator speaks through these Assistants, "down loading" these truths to us through our neutron path way, by way of the "baptism" of the Shekinah (one of the names many use to refer to the Holy spirit) which further opens one's "heart" to the "down pouring" of the light of understanding, wisdom, and love. I acknowledge all these and all "others" that guide, protect, heal, "teach" (remind) and assisted in my "awakening", AND, in yours. I am grateful to The Great Mystery Creator for my being created, and being here at this powerful time, and for all the assistance, guidance, and protection given in my existence. Without these loving gifts of light and love I would not be here on this Earth, nor would I have been able to make these books possible, thereby, extending the gifts to you and to life.

In EACH of the writings, my Spirit silently, yet, always gratefully, acknowledges the highest source of all life, along with all His/Her Spiritually high powers of light beings mentioned above. It is these purer beings of light that guide and assist us here on this plane of existence: Earth, Dimension Three. They help us to ascend into pure beings of light. It is because of their persistent desire to assist in the guidance and attempts to aid, not only me, but also, you, and all life forms, including other worlds/planets/dimensions, that I was able to bring these writings to you. Without them and their loving energy and persistent, yet patient and loving coaching, you would not be reading this book. Since it is then no accident that you came across this book, I must also thank them for guiding you to here. SECONDLY: I wish to acknowledge my gratefulness for having so many encourage me, in one way or another, to, as soon as possible, publish these writings for them and others, believing this can, and will aid others and the planet. I also thank those who took the time to read and comment on some of these writings. This was such an encouragement and inspiration, affirming to me, that I am meant to keep attuning, writing, and publishing. There have been so many of you, over the years, who I appreciate and wish to acknowledge, that I would not be able to list all your names and my gratitude to you on so few sheets of paper; but each of you know who you are. Know I thank each of you ***greatly and deeply*** *from my heart. You are many, and so I list not nearly enough of you that deserve to be listed; nor can I express strongly enough how valuable and instrumental you were in encouraging me in making it possible to get this completed. Thank you who openly encouraged me to do all that I could to get these writings out to the public. I list those from the first until I run out of space on this and the next two pages; but again, know, those of you who are not listed, are not forgotten, nor, no less recognized and appreciated. Again, Thank You Dear Ones!*

1. The unseen forces and events in my life: *which "called" to me, pulling me inward, where I responded to that beckoning call.*

2.* Miss Heyman: (my 5th grade teacher): *for the time in the year 1959. She had walked to my home after school one day, those many years ago, to ask my mother to encouraged me to write. She told my mother she'd seen a gift for writing in me...to my surprise! Even though my family never encouraged me, and I could not understand where she got that impression, the message stuck with me, making me contemplate on it every now and then. Thank you Miss Heyman!*

3.* The young woman across the street: *for the time in the year 1980: She came to my home, surprising me with her request for me to write a letter for her, "from her", to her husband, to save their marriage. She said she "felt" and believed I would know what to say which would make him "listen" and not leave her. I had not met her before.*

4.* My daughter Leah's kindergarten teacher: *for the time in the year 1984. She encouraged my daughter and me with her words: "have you mother write a book and you draw for it." She seen talent in Leah, and believed I had the gift of writing.*

5.* Alondra J. ("Tu-Tu"): *for: the time when she was in kindergarten, in the year 1983. She came to my home and asked me to help her write a Halloween story for class. When I asked her why she came to me, she said: "I don't know; I just feel you can do it."*

6.* A. Johnson: *(Medical receptionist/ health enthusiast), for: the time, in the year 1984, when she began coming to me, asking me to make cards with drawings and poetry-messages, expressing in them what she was feeling. She wanted to give them to a loved one. When I asked why me? She answered: "I don't know. I just felt you could do it and would be good at it."*

7.* Rose Printing Co.: (Their daughter): *for encouraging me with her words: In 1984 I had gone to her family's print shop to see about card stock and the printing of my own greeting cards. The owner's daughter, who worked there, had read some of my poems. She said she loved them, and I should put them in a book; if I did she wanted to buy it.*

***** *(None of these had ever heard me, nor heard anyone, speak of my being able to, nor desiring to ,write or draw. All of this got me to thinking and wondering if I had a "calling" to do these things.*** **Thank you for this!)**

8. Patrice Joy*: (intuitive, energy worker, light worker, spiritual teacher/speaker, for adults and children), for having me read my poetry to others by a fire, more then once. She encouraged me to publish them, and to write more.*

9. Fred H.: (In memory and appreciation of a Dear friend): *Spiritual student, seeker, furniture restorer): for respecting my beliefs; wanting me to publish my works; and encouraged me to follow my heart.*

10. Mike Cravens: *(Life student, singer, seeker, magician, and spiritual teacher: for the many times he asked me to read to him my poetry, telling others; asked me to publish my writings.*

11. Dr. Brenda W. PhD.: *(Author, filmmaker, producer, minister, life coach, T.V host): for offered her office and computer for me to write this book, and encouraged me to follow my dreams and mission.*

12. Chief Little Foot: *(Native American Story teller, seeker, spirit-messenger): for respecting, and believing in my intentions for the writings in this book. He listened to my writings while I read them, and encouraged me to have them published.*

13. Dr. Linda M.*: Family and children counselor, seeker): Read the book and told me she was impressed; I should publish; others could benefit from it.*

14. Horse Woman*: Faith keeper, energy healing worker, intuitive and visionary of the Leni Lanape, Native American Wolf Band in Ohio; wife of Chief Black Wolf), She encouraged me to publish; and told me about Author House.*

15. Scott and Karen Sullivan*: (Spiritual students, seekers. Karen: artist, crafter. Scott: Seeker), for donating a computer from Scott's work place, which the company, nor them, any longer wanted... (Even though I was unable to use it to type this book, it was a great inspiration towards getting the writings together and the book published!) * I also want to thank the company that switched to a later model, gifting the older one to the Sullivans, therefore, making it available for them to gift it to me.*

16. Dr. B. Hawks: *(Recognized Author, Native American energy worker, speaker, Teacher, seeker, minister, and intuitive, visionary): for his intuitive messages where he intuitively agreed to the publishing of this book and other books, and to continue my "healing" work for self and others; and for all his other encouragements.*

17. Judy "Running (Little) Cougar" Grooch*: (Seeker, healer, hobbyist of medicinal herbs): for her encouragement and respect.*

18. Haskell W.*: (Intuitive, wood & jewelry maker, "Gold-panner", dowser): for his faith and encouragement towards my publishing this book.*

19. Heather Weihi: *"The Faerie Lady". (She loves to make clay faeries; A artist,crafter, writer, and seeker) : for her words of encouragement to me.*

20.Teresa*Mahan:**(Intuitive,*Native*American*energy*worker,*dowser, researcher on medicinal herbs, seeker, Reiki Practitioner, member of The Friends of Serpent Mound): for listening to me read some of the writings from the book and her comments, and encouragement on this book and its publication.*

21. Bev McKenzie: *(Director of the Friends of Serpent Mound, dowser, intuitive, energy worker, and Girl Scout leader): for her listening to me read some of the writings from this book, her thoughts and her encouragement on this book and its publication, and for asking me to talk on my book at Serpent Mound.*
22. Kathleen T. (Spirit Wolf): *(Leni Lanape/Cherokee: seeker, intuitive, special needs social worker, beauty consultant, seamstress, jewelry maker, crafter, researcher on alterative health, and herbs): for her generous offer to use her home and computer if I needed, to get this book finished.*
23. Roberta Pignanelli: *(Seeker, visionary, cognitive and spiritual medicine dreamer, artist, jewelry maker, light worker. My fellow "Star Sister" and friend): for reading this book, when it was almost complete; then sharing with me how some of the writings took her far back, explaining some things to her, on a deeper level, assisting her. She encouraging me to finish and publish it. Thank you for being a good friend!*
24. Daniel and Anita B. *(Daniel: computer programmer, flute and musical instrument maker, Native American flute player, author, wood worker and designer; Anita: makes jewelry and natural care products of various kinds, artist): for the older lab top computer and Daniel's help with adobe. "I thank you both so much for this computer you no longer wanted! It enabled me to complete this book at home. This was so convenient, and saved me so much time. Thank you Daniel sooo very much for scanning my drawings so I could put them in this book and for all you've done to help. I would not have had this book ready for publishing at this time without your help! I cannot thank you both enough!* ***You both are "Angels"!***
25. Tina Marie: *For her desire to illustrate a drawing for the back of my book, using my vision for it while contributing her own details.*
***26. Belva Gregory**, *the Librarian who patiently helped me "work out the kinks in the machine." Thank you Belva!* **You are an Angel!** *I cannot express enough my gratitude. Your help was truly instrumental in my completing this book!*
27.** *I would also like to thank the* **Public library in B. Ohio** *for the use of their computers. Thanks to:* ***All those at the library who helped me!

****** A SPECIAL THANK YOU, to the little three year old girl-child for her gift of her blue crayon scribbling, in which I saw the wounded human; leading me to doing my Grandchildren's scribblings. I then did my own scribbles, adding those images to this book.**

You were *ALL* a great help! Truly, Thank YOU!

BOOK PREVIEW ABOUT THE AUTHOR

Dr. R. Lowery-Hawk was born on the Appalachians in Kentucky, and grew up in Ohio. She is a Doctor of Divinity; a Doctor of religious science; an ordained minister with a PhD. in religion; a mystic and a philosopher. She has been an initiate of six different mystery schools for close to forty years: four are Eastern based schools of the secret mysteries/philosophies of life, from different countries; and the other two are schools of Christian plus Native American philosophies and secret mysteries of life. She is a sensitive and empath; medium; ascension guide; and teacher of many modalities, with gifts of healing; intuitive medical; clairvoyance; vision; channeling; and akashia record reading. She is also an Author; poet; intuitive healer; counselor; and galactic messenger, having awakened and activated her pineal gland; channels; and her ancient and Divine DNA memories. Her "awakening" began over fifty-eight years ago, at the age of, or before, five.

Dr. R. Lowery-Hawk has written a number of books, including making meditation, visualization and spiritual teaching tapes. She has read some of her writings on three radio shows in Ohio, and one in North California, and has held workshops in Ohio, Kentucky and Indiana. She has a passion for, and has studied and researched: herbs; nature; holistic and alterative health; ancient religions; cultures; and various belief systems. She has also researched, with a great interest, other life enhancing, mind and conscience expansive studies. This includes the observing of life, self, and all creation, in a contemplative yet, reasoning state of mind. She has done this for close to forty years.

Dr. R. Lowery-Hawk's ancestry is of tsa-la-gi (Cherokee) and other Native America tribes; Belgium; German; and Irish/Scottish. She is single and lives in rural Ohio with her fur family: her dog-kids and cat-kids. She is currently working on making prints of the graphics, putting the books on Audio CD, and compiling her next book.

BOOK PREVIEW SUMMARY OF THE BOOK

Book One of The Books of "IS", is full of contemplative designs and graphics, along with rhythmic writings. All are created to move gently your senses, and your brain to "stirring" you "awake", and into thinking, sensing and observing life within you and around you. The writings and graphics are meant to be contemplated upon, and carried into your daily life, so to awaken you to the truth of you and the universe of life, in the here and now, and beyond the "here" and the "now". At the end of each chapter there are pages for the reader's own inspired writings brought on by the repeated reading, and contemplation of the writings and graphics. They are meant to assist in the activation of your creative and intellectual minds.

The writings in BOOK ONE: The Dance of Becoming are compiled messages and teachings from a higher presence of love which the Author received during a strong inter "calling" to write down what was "calling" to her. She began to realize that the writings were messages and memories of truth, guidance, and gentle love, coming forth from a higher Angelic Beings and other Divine Messengers and teachers. The Author realize that she must have been touching down into deeper parts of herself, and then rising up to her Higher Soul, her true Self, and then making contact with the hierarchy and Creator. Then, in the year 1984, she received a telepathic message by these Sacred Messengers of a higher power/creator, to put all these writings into a book, and when the time came, publish them to aid all mankind, all existence. That time has arrived!

The writings in this book and in the future Books of "IS", are "seed-truths" selectively and rhythmically placed, camouflaged, seeming at first, to those "not ready", as stories of mere fantasy, so called: "make-believe" and sci-fi. The writings are done this way so to gently but powerfully unlock the encoded truths within those who hear or read them and view the graphics. These writings therefore, are like camouflaged words/codes, hidden to many, but obvious to those who were "remembering", "awakened"; therefore, protected from those who would abuse them and misunderstand them in a negative way, creating too much chaos. The writings then, in the Books of "IS", are written in the forms of story, contemplative quotes, and poetic teachings, with various styles of poetry, delivering knowledge, Wisdom and understanding. This book's activation process is to assist in the "opening of the door" for: THOSE WHO SEEK TRUTH, AND SEEK THEMSELF. And, it is for: THOSE WHO ARE READY TO KNOW! That "door" opens to the All Knowing Universe of Truth, Wisdom, Knowledge and Understanding: THE KNOWING: The Book of Life/Records--- The Memories of Truth! These writings then, are "seeds", hidden, yet not, to those who have begun to awake and remember. "Seeds" of creation, hidden, yet there, awaiting:

"THOSE WHO ARE READY..."